DUMPSTERS AND
DIAMONDS

DUMPSTERS AND DIAMONDS

JACKIE HOLLAND

BRIDGE
LOGOS

Newberry, FL 32669

Bridge Logos, Inc.
Newberry, FL 32669

Dumpsters and Diamonds
By Jackie Holland

Copyright ©2017 by Bridge Logos, Inc.

Printed in the United States of America.

Library of Congress Catalog Card Number: 2016961791

International Standard Book Number: 978-1-61036-195-8

Unless otherwise noted Scriptures are taken from:

New King James Version®. (NKJV), Copyright © 1982 by Thomas Nelson. Used by permission. All rights reserved.
King James Version (KJV), public domain.
Amplified Bible (AMP), Copyright © , 1954, 1958, 1962, 1964, 1965, 1987 by The Lockman Foundation. Used by permission.

VP 12-21-16

You cannot know Jackie Holland very long without learning she has two great passions that direct her life. First of all, she loves Jesus with all her heart. Secondly, Jackie loves people. She loves people that many ministries overlook. She has a special gift of finding the diamonds in the rough.

SENIOR PASTOR RAYMOND ENGLAND
TRINITY LIGHTHOUSE CHURCH, DENISON TEXAS

In every generation God brings to the forefront someone who has been hidden away in obscurity. He uses one life, completely surrendered to Him, to channel His love and grace to a world in need. Jackie Holland is that "someone" of her generation.

SHARON BOLAN YERBY
SHARONBOLANYERBY.COM

I have known Jackie Holland for many years and I've seen up close her work with abused women. Jackie is the real deal. In an age of fakes and forgeries, she has been a true model of the compassion of Jesus Christ for countless people — and especially for the women she has rescued through her work in Dallas, Texas. Her story, which we published in Charisma magazine several years ago, is one of the most dramatic testimonies of Christ's redemption I've ever read. Her new book, Dumpsters and Diamonds, offers compelling proof that Jesus is alive today and working in His people.

J. LEE GRADY
FORMER EDITOR, CHARISMA MAGAZINE
DIRECTOR, THE MORDECAI PROJECT

It's an honor to call Jackie Holland a friend. She is one of the most genuine and enduring individuals I know. I've always loved how Jackie can see the beauty in the midst of some of the most difficult seasons of life. Her perspective comes from her deep and loving relationship with her heavenly father. You can't help feeling better about your issues when you're around Jackie. She is contagious!

STAN DENNIS
MARRIAGE & FAMILY PASTOR
GATEWAY CHURCH, NRH CAMPUS

Jackie Holland has been called to a unique ministry. At first I saw her diving in head first in that dumpster behind a grocery store to retrieve as she says,"Perfectly good food" to take back to our church and begin building one of the first major food ministries in the country.

From Dumpsters to Diamonds will guarantee a read that is intriguing, refreshing, humorous at times. In some stories the reader will be brought to a shocking halt, because of the riveting truth.

Jackie Holland is strikingly beautiful. She has the ability to go through doors holding her Bible to places very few other ministers could even get one foot in the door. Jackie has continued to take the Word to the lost... No matter the danger.

Jackie Holland has been called to a ministry reaching out especially to women who have lost their self respect and are being abused and don't know how to get out of their cage of pain. Other women are held captive behind bars...in prisons thinking they have no hope in their life. Jackie takes the message of Jesus directly to them in their den of darkness. Jackie Holland is the real thing! She has been my prayer sister for many years. We produced a television show aimed toward single women. Jackie Holland has a hunger as a minister to share the love of Jesus to hurting people who see no way out!

JAYNE BRANNON LYBRAND
AUTHOR, NON VERBAL COMMUNICATION CONSULTANT,
AUTHOR AND VOCAL AND STAGE PRESENCE COACH

I have never seen a heart to serve and meet the needs of people like I have seen in Jackie. It has been an honor to minister along side of her. She is an anointed woman of integrity.

KELLY WILHELMI
MINISTER CHILDREN'S ENTERTAINMENT

"Triumphant would be the one word to chronicle the life of Jackie Holland. She relentlessly transmutes tragedy into a testimonial for God's Glory! If anyone could understand the powerful transformation of 'Dumpsters to Diamonds' — it would definitely be our beloved Jackie Holland — because she's lived it!"

JEREMIAH & MARGURITTE JOHNSON
THEHELPSTUDIOS

ACKNOWLEDGEMENTS

Love and kisses to Charlsey Popp and Howard Holland, my precious adult children, always there for me. I know the Lord knows who to put in families and I truly cherish my children and their children and families.

I thank God for Elaine and Woodrow Jackson, my parents, who trained us up to love the Lord and they lived their lives being wonderful examples of faith in Christ.

Charlsey has continually encouraged me to go forward with completion of this book. She would say you can do it, Mom, I know you can. I think I stretched her a bit but she has books in her that will need to come out one day. She described me as bigger than life. Charlsey is married to Jeff who has been so supportive of her and he never seems to mind our long talks on the phone. I thank God for my grandson Isaiah Bock and he and Brittany's two children, my great grandchildren Bearon and Scarlett.

Howard, my son, is also my best friend. I am so thankful he is not ashamed to say he loves his Mom and wants me to be happy and well and do the ministry God called me to do.

Howard has three beautiful daughters Cierra, Alexis, and Dallas, all very beautiful like their Mother and Father. He watches over me well, thank you Howard.

I thank God for the love and support of my brother Don Jackson and his wife Deann, my sister Barbara and her husband Coach Bottoms and my sister Marita and her husband Harold

Roden. I love my family and their families so much. I love my step children and hold them near my heart.

My very special thanks and appreciation to Kirie and Jimmy James for believing in me and this book enough to make it happen financially. You are too wonderful for words.

Susan Reddick my friend and assistant for over 25 years, has been such a blessing and help to me. Thank you, Susan.

For all my ministry partners, volunteers and co-laborers in ministry who have so faithfully stood with me over these past 29 years in full time ministry. If I should list them all it would be too long but each of you know the sacrifices made on my behalf and I pray God blesses you all back 100 fold. Your prayers, your calls and financial support have kept me going strong even when the times were so very hard. Thank you from the bottom of my heart. I thank God for the opportunity to serve in the Jail.

And I never fail to mention the sweet presence of the Holy Spirit guiding and leading me each day. I thank God for his wonderful son Jesus who paid the penalty for our sins and by faith and his grace in him made eternal life possible for all believers alike.

INTRODUCTION

I am so excited to get this book completed and in your hands. Nothing is ever a one man show, it truly takes teamwork to make dreams work. God knows who, why, when and where the connections are to your destiny and life assignment. It is nothing less than a miracle from God. I had been on TBN doing a interview and a man named Robb Ellis called me from Grand Rapids, Michigan. He had been a professional baseball player and had written several sports books then became a licensed counselor. He watched the interview and sensed the Lord say "she needs a book and you need to help her." He called, made plans, drove down and did one on one interviews with me and he did a fine job. However, my friend Tamra Vines said, "Jackie, I want to help you write your book, I know you well and I sense the Lord say 'do it for you'."

We completed it after a few months, and I called Carol Stertzer who had written an interview with me for Charisma magazine and asked who she might suggest as an editor for my book. She gave me a list of names and I chose Marsha Ford. That was over 17 years ago when I sent her my manuscript. She called and said, "I have a Publisher I do some work for. I would like to send them your manuscript if that's okay." Of course, I was excited, I had never had written a book before and I had no knowledge how difficult it is for the most excellent well known writers to get their manuscripts looked at!

Guy Morrell was the Publisher of Bridge Logos. He called one day and with his beautiful British accent said, 'Jackie, the girls here in the office really like your book and we would like to publish it for you...' I went on and on about how grateful I was and how I felt that the Lord had given me the book to get my story out to the public. He said that he sensed clearly that the Lord had directed him to publish this book for me. Would you believe I met Guy Morrell and his daughter Suzi for the first time in New Orleans at the Christian Booksellers Convention and saw my beautiful completed book *Exposed Heart* and met two of the finest people on the face of the earth.

My best friend, Laquetta Dinsmore, traveled with me and we had such a marvelous time. I remember Guy saying not all books make money. Naturally he said, "we are a business and want to make money but ministry is our heart. We believe your story needs to be told."

Sixteen difficult years have passed. One day I was sitting at my desk at the Upscale Thrift store we have in Sherman Texas and I had a thought to call Florida and see if Suzi ever came to that place. We were completely out of touch. I knew Guy had passed away a few years prior and she lived in the UK. When I called the Bridge Logos office I asked the secretary if Suzi ever came there. She said, "Yes, she is here but on the other line." I said, "Well just tell her Jackie Holland who had the book *Exposed Heart* had called. She need not return the call but just tell her hello for me."

Within minutes the phone rang and it was Suzi Wooldridge! Oh, it was so good to hear her voice. I told her how much her Dad meant to me and how grateful and thankful I was that he believed in me and published my book.

We discussed the possibility of revising *Exposed Heart* and after a couple of weeks I was feeling well enough to start working on the book. In my heart I thought how odd and difficult to attach those last 16 years to the end of my book. I kept it in my heart and did not mention what I was thinking. Suzi emailed me the next morning and asked how I felt about doing a brand-new book. Well, this is how I felt, elated, happy, joyful, shocked, grateful, thankful, and again excited!

So here we are with *Dumpsters and Diamonds*, my story told from my heart to yours. I hope and pray this book will provide comfort, healing, hope and joy to your heart. The Lord spoke to my heart when I had been diagnosed with stage 4 cancer and said, "you shall live, not die but declare the works of the Lord." That was 3 years ago, cancer not active, no treatments. Thank you, Suzi Wooldridge, President of Bridge Logos Publishing for making this dream a reality. Guy Morrell and Laquetta Dinsmore along with so many of our loved ones are perhaps cheering us on from a distance.

DEDICATION

*Dumpsters and Diamonds is dedicated in honor of
Guy Morrell and my friend Laquetta Dinsmore.*

CONTENTS

LET THE PARTY BEGIN

One of my all time favorite stories in the Bible is the one of the prodigal son. You know, the one like some of us were, stubborn spoiled and rebellious, wanting our way and wanting everything today, it had to be today! Well, that young man had a great inheritance in store for him and his brother, but he just could not wait so he said, "Father, I want my portion now, I have dreams and I am going to do great things in life not just sit around here until I am too old to enjoy myself." He kept pestering his dad until he gave in like so many of us have done with our own children; they win you over because they wear you down. You hope they make it but somewhere in the pit of your stomach you are thinking 'God, have mercy.'

Sin always promises us more than it gives, takes you further than you want to go and leaves you worse off than you were before. After four failed marriages, the first beginning at only 15 years old, I have experienced so many heartbreaks and disappointments in life. I remember one particular day going to a garage sale, and I bought a music cassette for my mother. I drove a short distance remembering the cassette. I thought, 'I will see if it works', so popped it in the player...Oh my Lord, it broke my heart as I listened to the words, simply saying 'God is calling you home.'

I pulled over to the side of the road and cried my eyes out. I wanted to go back to the safety of my Heavenly Father's home and once again feel the shelter of his arms. I wanted to feel clean and free from the dirt that had hardened my heart.

I have heard the expression 'you can not shack up with the devil and expect God to pay the rent!' Rebellion in the heart is totally self-centered. Only when the Lord opens our eyes to see do we realize the damage and pain we inflicted on others who loved us.

Music that is wrapped in the anointed words of love can pierce the hardest hearts. I feel certain my mother had cried many tears and prayed many prayers for me and wasn't it sweet of the Lord to use a dollar music tape, purchased for her, to break my hard, cold heart?!

The older brother rushed into the house after hearing the loud music and said, "What is this? Are you giving my sorry brother a party? I have worked hard and never wasted my life and you are giving him a party...unbelievable; I have never had a party. I should have lived like the devil myself. Look at me. I have wasted my years by doing what was right."

The father answered, "No, my son. All that I have is yours but your brother was dead and now he is alive it is right to give him a party." Sadly the older brother did not see it the same way and he would carry anger and bitterness in his heart.

Certainly my brother and sisters were happy to see that my life had changed for the better, but without ever saying a word they may have felt irritated that our parents always welcomed me back with open arms, giving me another chance and forgiveness, like nothing had ever happened. I was the baby girl once again. Never give up on your loved ones. They may fail over and over again. Just keep on believing and one day you will see a new person.

A mother is crying out for her child…young or an adult needing help, just the same. Addictions, strongholds, disappointments and deep despair. No, no, no, not again, dear Lord. They are living on the edge, now wondering, hoping, praying that something will change, that things will get better.

Will the prodigal son or daughter make it this time? You see on their face the disappointment and the deep despair, hearing the words from their own mouth, broken, feeling rejected; saying, God is not there. Jesus is not there. He will not help me.'

It is absolutely the most painful and tragic way any parent or loved one can live. Both the one with the addictions and the one who cares deeply for the one with the addiction, both are pulled into the pit wondering when it will ever stop. Let go of what you can… but never stop praying and believing for their total recovery.

The Bible says if one sows to the wind they will reap a whirlwind. Let's be honest, there is pleasure in sin for a season.

There are consequences to our actions, and sometimes it hurts badly. Jesus said, "the physician does not come for the well, but the sick."

Pray, pray, and love. If you forsake your children in their time of despair, Satan will continue doing his best to destroy their lives. We must be willing to shift the prayers to 'not my will but yours be done' for the prodigal. Ask God for the grace to be strong but love unconditionally.

The older brother had a self righteous attitude and a heart of bitterness. He felt overlooked and not appreciated. He needed assurance and understanding. God forgives; be thankful. If you were in their position that grace extended would be wonderfully received.

There are effects of past drug and alcohol abuse. Most people need structure and counsel. I would encourage you to get into a group or find someone who cares and listens but you must allow them to speak into your life. Humble yourself under the mighty hand of God and he will lift you up.

If God is for us he is enough and who can be against us? Please God, put him first. Others will just have to get in line. You are his beloved so just enjoy your party; celebrate your recovery and your relationship with the Father. No shame, no disgrace. Eat, drink and be merry. No condemnation. Your Heavenly Father is rejoicing and happy to have you home!

SCRIPTURE PROMISE

For by grace are you saved through faith, not of works lest any man should boast.

— EPHESIANS 2:8-9

PRAYER

Heavenly Father, we thank you for giving us these comforting words of promise and hope for the future. Today with all my tasks ahead and all the trials or tests I might encounter, I put my trust and faith in you. I know deep in my heart you love me and care for me and all that concerns my life and future. Thank you for leading me out of a hopeless life and taking me into a new way of life and allowing me to see and feel the hope and light of your love. Thank you, Lord, for giving us free salvation not by works but faith in you alone. We trust you now. We agree nothing is too hard for the Lord. Father, thank you, we can trust you with those we love and we believe for recovery and healing, body, soul and spirit. Amen.

BREAKING THE CURSE OF SUICIDE
(CHARLSEY'S STORY)

I was sitting in a hotel room in Mobile Alabama working claims with my husband when I got the call. It was in the morning… and as I looked and read the caller ID of my cell phone, I was surprised. It was my Mom….she asked me, "What I was doing?" as she has done in a thousand phone calls before. Little did I know today's call would be different. I said we were waiting to go into a meeting and she said, "Charlsey, I have some bad news about your Daddy."

I felt my hand grip the phone a little tighter as I could hear her bracing me for something important. "Your Daddy is dead. They think he shot himself", she said. A rush of horror crossed my mind. I sat down on the edge of the bed and began to cry. Shocked…In total disbelief that he was gone. He was gone and I did not get the chance to say, "Good-bye". We ended our phone call and I relayed all that was told to me to my husband.

I took a plane and headed to Texas. I called my college aged son who was on a break at that time and was available to go with me. Just think, a school break in April. Talk about timing.

He would drive us from my home in Texas to the small town of Avery, Texas, where Daddy lived.

My son and I had a 2 ½ hour drive. We are both lovers of music and have always shared that together. How odd that on that day in *this* car ride we would be choosing the songs for my daddy's, his granddaddy's funeral. We chose songs about strong men...men with broken lives. The words to each song completely described my dad.

He was once tall dark and handsome, a cowboy who felt most at home on the back of a big beautiful horse. He wore a Stetson with pride and a pair of boots with delight. Honestly, for all his short comings he was a man's man. A man who had turned gray, was depressed and took his life one lonely evening. Depression can rob even the strongest man of his joy.

I entered the house of my aunt who could fill me in on the details that she knew up to Daddy's death. Up to that point I didn't know he had shot and killed himself for sure. A truth that was almost more painful than I could bear. As the tears rolled down my face...I sat calmly and listened...in a blur all I could think about was *Mike*, my older beloved brother who had taken his own life years before (my daddy's son).

My aunt told me that Daddy was in the process of moving into the house next door to her. She said he had been depressed. She had not gone into the house. She said she couldn't do it. In fact, other than the police who kicked down the door and found him, *no one* had been in the house. Since I could not see Daddy I *wanted* and *needed* to go into *that* house.

Amazing, the strength God gives us when we find we need it the most. The door had been knocked down but the police had fixed it so no one could go in and there was yellow caution tape everywhere. I remember turning to my son and saying, "you don't have to go in, but I do." I will go in and come back for you. I just have to see for myself first. I knew he was worried about me but at that point he knew he could not stop me.

We managed to get the door open and I was able to climb through a small opening. My son turned and stood by the car. Having never been in this house its layout was unfamiliar to me. The first room I walked into had a closet and the closet door was open. First I saw *Daddy's* clothes. He always had the starch pressed shirts that every real cowboy seems to own and at the bottom of the closet *his* boots. I had to pull myself together. I had to be strong. I kept walking until I came to the next bedroom. That's where I froze.

There in front of me were two twin beds. The one on the right was obviously where my daddy took his life. Under my breath I cried, "Dear Jesus, please help me." The top mattress was separated from the bottom where his body obviously had been. From the impact of the gunshot wound to his head, his body had slid off the mattress. There he was in was a pool of blood...and when my eyes fell upon it I dropped to my knees.

My son stood in the doorway of the bedroom and we surveyed the room together. After a brief few moments I said to my son, "Daddy was such a private person. I *have* to clean this up...this is a small town where gossip can travel fast and the story can grow from what it is now." He watched as I took additional towels and wet them and began to clean up the puddle of blood from Daddy's body.

While I was cleaning the blood, I prayed particularly for my son and my younger brother. I pleaded the blood of Jesus over them that NO SUICIDE would come to my family again and I felt the Lord tell me, "No more", and that peace has stayed with me from that day until now. We never know how strong we are until we are truly tested.

When I watched my mother go through the steps of my brother's death I really did not understand her strength but I witnessed a similar strength in my own life when Daddy was buried. If you know someone struggling with depression encourage them to reach out for help.

Thank you, Charlsey, for sharing this story and experience with us. It is true gut ministry and the greatest thing you can do for someone depressed is to share this story with them. My prayer is that it will keep them from going over the edge and they will reach out and ask for help. I think the greatest tribute to a man would be for his daughter to share her heart with others like Charlsey has in this book and then at least his experience is not in vain but will be life giving.

SCRIPTURE PROMISE

For I know the plans I have for you declares the Lord, plans for welfare and not for evil to give you a future and a hope.

— JEREMIAH 29:11)

PRAYER

Dear Heavenly Father, I pray you touch the heart of the readers and they feel the love and care that is given here. Lord, as much as we can humanly love, your love is so much deeper and richer than anyone on earth has ever experienced. You loved the whole world so much that you gave your son to be a ransom for so many. Thank you, Jesus, for coming to earth, living and experiencing our hurts and pain. You know and you understand and then you took all that shame, pain and blame on yourself and paid for our sins. We accept Jesus as Lord and Savior and our only hope of a home in heaven. We love you. Amen.

3

KEYS TO THE KINGDOM

A major key that opened up a new world for me…Shaking back and forth like electricity moving throughout my body, I had given in to the power of the Holy Spirit. I thought, I know I look crazy but I also know God is doing a work in my life, and I did not want to miss this moment… I was in Kansas city at a conference with Mahesh Chavda and he said there is a great Revival coming around Dallas Fort Worth and you will be a part of it, also changes with Roe versus Wade will come out of that place (Texas). There was no way this man would have known I lived in the DFW area which was several hours drive from Clarksville where I was born. The key for me was, do I believe this man is speaking a word from God?

My marriage was horrible and I prayed every day that it would change, that my husband would become a good Christian man. He said he was, but his life sure did not seem that way. In those days I had discovered the ministry of James Robison. He held crusades for years and reached millions. In one particular conference my life was deeply touched and changed.

My husband had been gone a month or so on a trip and I was to pick him up at the DFW Airport when he arrived; but, I had attended a conference near there at that time. I remember the ministry time was so amazing that when at the end of the service someone just calmly walked by and laid their hands on me, I went flat on my back. I did not feel it physically but spiritually I was touched by the power of God.

I remember thinking, this is crazy. I had come from a Baptist background and had grown up going to charismatic services but in my heart had always judged the falling part, thinking to myself... now that could be avoided and was unnecessary... Key here: let God be God and do not question him. I needed help and I was very open to a visitation from the Lord.

I lay there just crying out to God and saying, "I am so sorry I thought this was fake." The "feeling" was exhilarating and I was praying, 'Lord, here I am. Send me!' I meant it with all my heart. After a bit, I got up and remembered I had missed the time of picking up my husband. I rushed out and drove quickly to the airport.

My heart was pounding and fear was rising in my heart. I knew he would be furious. Sure enough he was standing there, bags in hand and I was petrified. He threw his bags into the back seat and made some sound under his breath like a growl but did not speak a word to me on the way home. I had no way of knowing these were the last days we would ever be together.

All the way I was praying, 'don't let him hurt me, Lord. I plead your blood over my life, I am in your hands'... When we arrived home he grabbed his bags, went in and still never said a word. The Lord had shut his mouth and even though he was angry, I knew the devil wanted him to beat the hell out of me but it was as though he was bound!

That very week-end I discovered my husband was living a double life and the girl he was living with was pregnant. He divorced me. God in his mercy was already preparing my heart and opening my spiritual eyes and ears to obey and follow him for the rest of my days.

Domestic violence and four failed marriages. Who am I going to blame for that? No one twisted my arm and forced me into those marriages. I just made some really bad choices when it came to love relationships. I have remained single now over 29 years. Apparently, I figured it all out, everyone is not meant to be married but everyone is called to serve the Lord.

I love the story of Elijah the prophet in 1 Kings where God had told him to go to a certain brook where he would find food and water. This was in the time of a great drought. One day the brook dried up, and God told him to go see a widow who would feed him. So he went to her home and said, "fix me something to eat." She said, "I am getting ready to fix my son and me our last food. This is all we have, so after this is gone we will die." She showed hospitality and gave the prophet food and by doing so God gave a blessing to her. Little did she know when she obeyed that was a provisional key for her future.

When we are at the end of our rope just tie a knot and hang on, because when God gets ready to bless you nothing can stop that blessing. Obedience is our key to advancement and promotion. Sometimes it is sacrificial giving and serving, but it is almost always waiting, and going through hard times and barren places before the brook starts flowing again. Here is your key... don't give up. God is not through using you!

SCRIPTURE PROMISE

> *For I am persuaded beyond doubt* (am sure) *that neither death nor life, nor angels nor principalities, nor things impending and threatening nor things to come, nor powers, nor height nor depth, nor anything else in all creation will be able to separate us from the love of God which is in Christ Jesus our Lord.*

> — ROMANS 8:38, 39

PRAYER

Dear Heavenly Father, we thank you for your favor and your grace. Thank you for showing us your way. Only in you do we find the way, the truth and the life. Lord, you are the key to our happiness, our forgiveness, our hope and future. Bless the one reading this right now and show them clearly you are the key they have searched for in days gone by. You said if we confess that Jesus is Lord you hear us and direct us along life's way. We need your guidance and help. Thank you for hearing our prayers and loving us despite our past actions, sins and mistakes. Amen.

4

THE PRINCESS BRIDE

Susan, my assistant and good friend, reminisced about her daughter Jennifer's wedding that, to me, revealed a facet of God's "Mother" heart.

Jackie arrived at the house and before you know it, she had Jennifer in the bathroom, gelling, styling, curling, and teasing. She teased Jennifer's hair up, set that dainty little tiara firmly in place, and applied false eyelashes and more makeup to Jennifer. Jennifer slipped on the earrings and in a few short minutes she looked like a princess! A princess bride!

Jennifer and her fiancé, Matt, decided for the sake of the student loan forms to get married the summer before school started that Fall. When I spoke with Jennifer about it, she expressed the desire to just go to the Justice of the Peace. My reply was, "Jennifer, I think we could do a real nice wedding for you and Matt at the house - you would be able to have your family and friends there - and I believe we could make some really nice memories."

Jennifer agreed and so for the next four weeks Andy and I furiously worked to get the house ready for the wedding. That was a blessing in itself to me because we had many unfinished projects around the house that needed to be finished. We had just put them off so now we were getting them all completed. The house was really transformed and at night with all the white twinkling lights and candles reflecting in the mirrors framed by walls painted Opera House red it all looked so special and elegant. I was also praying through it all, sharing my heart with the Lord, that I so wanted the wedding to be a special event and be a blessing to Jennifer and Matt, Matt's family, and my family.

As soon as I found out that Jennifer and Matt were getting married I asked Jackie if she would perform the ceremony. She so graciously accepted - I couldn't imagine anyone else other than Jackie doing the ceremony! I decided on a menu, and contacted the family members. By the night before the wedding I was running out of steam. Jennifer picked out her outfit - a tasteful sea foam green silk suit. On the day of the wedding there were so many things to do. All of the food preparation had to be done that morning. We served cold foods, fruit, cheese, sliced meats, chicken salad, cold punch. Because it was a hot Texas summer I had to wait to set out the food until the last possible minute so it would all be cold and fresh.

Jennifer began to get ready that afternoon. She put on her make-up and curled her hair. It was warm and muggy that day and her hair would hardly hold a curl. It was too curly to be straight and too straight to be curly. She did the best she could but she just wasn't looking very bridal. She was getting frustrated. I felt sad. I didn't know what to do. Jennifer's hair has always been hard to manage.

I tried to help but it didn't do much good. I went back to the kitchen to finish washing up some dishes. As I was standing at the sink with a sad heart I began to pray, "Father, I just wish Jennifer could look bridal but I don't know what to do! We have run out of time!" You know all the preparations are great but on the wedding day everyone's eyes are on the bride!

Well, the Lord does everything very well! He sent his servant to save the day! Jackie was at her house just getting ready to step out the door. She was standing at her dresser picking out some earrings. Her eyes fell to a tiara decorated with rhinestone hearts sitting on her dresser. The thought occurred to her, "I'll just take this along, and maybe Jennifer can use it in her hair." Then, her eyes fell on a pair of hoop earrings, "Maybe these will look cute on Jennifer, I'll just take these along, too! Why don't I take my make-up case with me just in case Jennifer needs a little help with her make-up?"

Jackie arrived and before you know it she had Jennifer in the bathroom, gelling, styling, curling, and teasing. She teased Jennifer's hair up, set that dainty little tiara firmly in place, and applied false eyelashes and more make-up to Jennifer. Jennifer slipped on the earrings and in a few short minutes she looked like a princess! A princess bride! When I went to check on them I was so surprised to see the transformation! I exclaimed, "Jennifer, you look like a princess! I could tell Jennifer felt like a princess!" This is exactly what a bride should feel like on her wedding day!

Jennifer took the fragrant stargazer lily and white rose bouquet her mother-in-law had designed for her and walked down our small hallway to her groom while two of our friends from church played flute and guitar instrumentals. Jennifer and Matt were joined in holy matrimony before their family and friends. My prayers were answered over what I could have asked. My family went on and on for days reminiscing about how wonderful their wedding had been and how beautiful and happy Jennifer and her beloved looked that night.

A wedding can be the most exciting and yet the most stressful time in the bride to be and the families' lives. So many choices to make. Will it be small or large? How much money can we spend? What is my theme? All the way to which guests will be invited. Many people go deep in debt trying to provide that beautiful wedding. We want them to have more than we had in life.

I want to go back for minute to a wedding of great importance in Jesus' life. During the festivities, they ran out of wine...Jesus' mother told him they were out of wine, so Jesus turned the pots of water into wine...but not just any old wine. He saved the best for last. This was Jesus' first miracle at a wedding. I think of Susan and her heartfelt prayer to God regarding her daughter Jennifer and as always, God, you granted the desires of a mother's heart.

SCRIPTURE PROMISE

O God, You are my God, earnestly will I seek you; my inner self thirsts for You, my flesh longs and is faint for You, in a dry and weary land where there is no water.

— PSALM 63:1

PRAYER

Dear Heavenly Father, I thank you for loving your daughters and your sons. It seems to me you take a special interest in preparing your daughters for their wedding and their future. You love them and they need to remember that no matter what troubles, trials or disappointments you see them as beautiful daughters. All of us Christians will one day sit with you at the wedding supper and even the most beautiful weddings we have ever seen or witnessed will not compare to our wedding with you. We are your beloved and you are our desire. Amen.

5

REVIVE US AGAIN

Everybody wants to go to Heaven but nobody wants to die! The old saying, 'You cannot ride to Heaven on Daddy's coat tails' is true. Or the one that says, 'Grandma may pray you into seminary but she can't get you into Heaven.' Mama called and Daddy sent will not get you through those pearly gates. You must make the decision on your own.

In Psalm 85:6 it says, 'Will you not revive us again that your people may rejoice in you?' Salvation is a beautiful gift and God does not force himself on us. Actually if we could not make choices or decisions ourself it would be much easier. But that is not what grace and true faith and forgiveness is about.

I was in my thirties and had a desire to share my faith but was too afraid and insecure. The church I was attending began a study called "Evangelism Explosion" which was basically learning how to introduce people young and old alike to the saving knowledge of Jesus Christ... Soul Winning! I had read the scripture that said, 'Do not fear what you will say. When the opportunity arises just open your mouth and the Holy Spirit will give you the words when needed.'

I had practiced the questions on my 17 year old daughter for about three days. I was getting myself geared up to go out and knock on doors with my team and do some soul winning. I asked her the question, 'If you were to die right now, Charlsey, why would God say he would let you get into his Heaven?'

She began to cry and totally broke down sobbing; she said he would not let her in. Then she added, 'I want to be saved.' Charlsey had always been in church and had known about the Lord but right at that moment I was shocked when she was so broken, and I think even then I thought maybe she just thinks she was not saved.

I remembered the time when my sister Barbara had taken my children to her church? I suppose she asked what they thought of the service and did they know Jesus as their Savior? Mike began to cry and said, "I want to be saved", and then my sister asked Charlsey, "are you saved?". She readily agreed, "I want to also be saved too."

She pulled into the Safeway grocery store parking lot and prayed with them right there. She led them in prayer that night and I do remember them sharing with me because Mike was so happy about that prayer…but now Charlsey admitted during our practice evangelism session she had really never thought through salvation but she had tried to be a good girl.

My children had their own motorcycles, so that is how she would go to school or run errands for me. Charlsey admitted later that God had really been dealing with her heart regarding the question that I had asked her. She said she did not ride the bike for three days but instead walked to the school. She was afraid she might have a wreck and not be ready to die. She was 17 and God brought her to the moment and place where she fell on her knees. I kneeled right beside her and she asked Jesus into her heart as Lord and Savior.

Revival is when God's people return to him with their whole heart. We must decrease, he must increase. Revival occurs when God's people recognize him as Lord and Saviour in their life. Jesus alone is more than enough when you have that first love feeling and experience with him. Revival services have their place, but unless the focus becomes all about Jesus and not about us, we have not truly been revived.

Only a consuming revival fire can save us now from anything, no sin too dark, no crime too horrid, no pit too deep. We need God's fire to burn up our self-centered ways, and our need for the approval of man.

I remember in the 1980's being challenged by President Ronald Reagan to be the year of the Bible. He challenged everyone to read the Word daily that year, and so I took the challenge. Before I would read a little here and there if it fitted or made sense of whatever was going on in my life at the time. With that commitment, changes come to our life.

Someone once asked, 'how far do we go to reach a soul?' No trouble too great, no humiliation too deep, no suffering too severe, no love too strong, no labor too hard, no expense too great but it is worth it all to win just one soul. God loves the world; he sent his son…

Proverbs 11:30:

He that wins souls is wise.

The Bible says the angels rejoice over just one sinner that repents.

Repent is not a dirty word...Both John the Baptist and Jesus began their public ministries by calling for God's people to repent. Revival stirs the hearts of others to want to hear the message of repentance. Obedience and passion come from revival. We come to God admitting our need and weakness and we need his strength and power and anointing to change. That is repentance.

SCRIPTURE PROMISE

"If my people who are called by my name will humble themselves and pray and seek my face and turn from their wicked ways, then I will hear from Heaven, I will forgive their sins, and I will heal their land."

— 2 CHRONICLES 7:14

PRAYER

Dear Heavenly Father, today I commit my life to you again. Here I am Lord. Just as I am I come. Teach me your ways, Lord, so that I will not sin against you. Thank you for providing a way out of sin and death...You sent your son Jesus to live on earth and go through temptations, pain, rejection and death. He shed his own blood to pay for my sins. He died, rose again and now is sitting at your right hand in Heaven hearing my prayer. Create in me a clean heart, O God and renew a right spirit within me. You said if we confess our sins, you are faithful and just to forgive us our sins and cleanse our heart from all unrighteousness. Today I can boldly confess I receive Jesus as my Lord and Savior. Yes, I am yours, Lord. Revive me again! Amen.

6

SPIRITUAL GIFTS

Imagine right now, you are sitting in the middle of a "Great Big World Pot." You are amazed that the Father himself is beginning to stir up the contents of what is in your pot. You may be sensing agitation, and everything inside begins to roll around. In desperation when the heat is turned up everything ugly starts rising to the top. Ouch, it hurts, stop. I don't want to go there, I will deal with those things another day. Yet something cries out from deep within, and you say, 'I am desperate for help. Father, have mercy on me, I need change in my life and I cannot do it alone.'

You have walked in a hard place too long. Your time has come. You have many gifts and God has given you creative ideas to help enhance, not just your own life, but to help others succeed and become all that he intended them to be. Most time we disregard and do not act on implementing those ideas.

God even gives witty inventions and ideas to ordinary men and women who can solve a problem. It is very probable you will sense those creative juices flowing again. Let the Father guide you and show you his abundant love, provision and grace and think outside of that box.

God gives us dreams and visions, beginning first as just a "seed of an idea." When that seed is planted into a fertile heart of faith and hope, then sacrifice and hard work, maybe even tears, in due time it will take root and those dreams can become your reality. Don't give up. The best is yet to come.

Most people seem to like prophetic words...but you must learn to be as wise as a serpent and harmless as a dove. The reason we are talking about gifts is we all have been given gifts from God but we must know how and when to use them. We need to know their purpose. We have not been blessed with these gifts just to set on a shelf and look pretty. Discernment is extremely important.

People around you are hurting and need what you have to offer. You are much more equipped than you know. We just ask God to stir up those gifts right now...then you will do exploits... signs and wonders and speak on his behalf, making his name known throughout the world.

Aren't you glad we are not all alike? That would be very boring, I think. But we are different, unique some a bit more on the edge than others. You may be thinking right now, 'this is making me nervous. I do not want to do anything out in public.' Trust me, if he calls he equips so don't concern yourself on how when or where, just be a good receiver!

All of us together are Christ's body, and each of us is a part of it. God has appointed for the church: first apostles, prophets, teachers, those who do miracles, those who have the gift of healing, and those who can help others, those who have the gift of leadership, and those who speak in unknown languages.

Are we all apostles? Are we all prophets? Are we all teachers? Do we all have the power to do miracles? Do we all have the gift of healing? Do we all have the ability to speak in unknown languages? Do we all have the ability to interpret unknown languages? Of course not! So, you should desire the most helpful gifts. Just love God first and others as yourself.

I don't think you have to struggle with finding your assignment; just be concerned with the needs of others. What is your passion? What excites your interests and causes you to listen when the subject comes up? You will find that God has anointed you to do those things already. The Holy Spirit leads you and guides you into all truth.

Pastor Doug White wanted everyone involved in the ministry. I remember him saying, 'if I show up at church and no one is here but visitors because all the regulars are out doing ministry that makes me happy.' You can tell how strong the church is when you see how spiritually strong the people are, not only the pastors. That is why he gives gifts to all of us. We should never covet other's gifts but just do our best with what we have been given.

Remember, every good and perfect gift is from above. God gives good gifts to man. Let's agree and say, 'Lord, use my gifts and let me be a blessing in my family and reach out into my community.' No gift is small but great in the sight of the Lord. He is stirring them up right now. Just lift your hands and say, 'here am I Lord. Have your way in my life.'

SCRIPTURE PROMISE

The Lord is gracious and full of compassion, slow to anger and abounding in mercy and loving-kindness. The Lord is good to all, and His tender mercies are over all His works [the entirety of things created].

— PSALM 145: 9, 10

PRAYER

Dear Heavenly Father, I know you love me and I love you. Thank you for equipping me to do your work and the ability to stay strong in my faith. Jesus, you are a perfect example for us to follow. Show us the way and help us walk in your way.

My life is yours. Fill me with your Holy Spirit, I pray. Amen.

WOMEN IN MINISTRY

Sister Girls, I will tell you up front; we are all that and a bag of chips.... If you do not believe I am great as I say, just ask me! Raising my voice to a higher level I must prove myself and try and compete every day in a man's world. I have struggled to get noticed and acknowledged for my many attributes. Actually, I am angry as hell and I am not going to take it anymore.

No, just kidding; that is not true...but that is how many women in ministry are perceived by men and other women. Knowing this gives us an edge. We must be wise as serpents and harmless as doves. We must walk softly and carry a big stick! We must remember that it has only been a few years since a woman could vote, much less be a preacher or have a ministry. In the old days there was a great gulf fixed... within the boundaries of Sunday schools or women's ministries. We are not in competition!

I am a woman, so I have a basic understanding of women. I am not speaking as an intellectual scholar or teacher but as a woman who has been on the front lines for 29 plus years. It is called experience, learning the hard way.

This is what I want to say regarding my sisters just starting out in ministry. Put your big girl panties on and strap yourself in because ministry will take you on the ride of your life.

True, you may have been overlooked but that is by man, not God.

Now, I say this with love and experience. My dear sister, just give it all back over to the Lord. No point in crying, kicking or screaming. That only makes people think you want pity or vengeance. Sister, more will be accomplished by your hard work, ethics, integrity and calm spirit than by being at that right place at that right time to get the right attention.

The devil wants to humiliate you and make you feel unworthy. Do not let that happen. You tell the devil to get behind you because you want the things of God. One caution on this matter is woman/man in counseling sessions; many times, these have opened the door to sinful actions. Watch and be alert. People who are hurting can sometimes be drawn to you as the person of their dreams. Don't go there. Remember your calling and stay firm in faith.

Guard against criticism, blame and justification of self, such as complaining about employees or past employers. Just be your sweet self and give yourself room to grow. People need to hear the message burning in your heart, straight, simple, honest, direct and covered in love.

In my heart I knew I was called into the Christian ministry. But without the education and training how on earth could I ever accomplish anything for God? God was merciful to me and allowed my ministry to start in a dumpster and it grew to having different locations, even in Laundromats at apartment complexes. You notice I did not say in other cities. Bloom where you are planted. When you help hurting people the word gets around quickly.

It did not take a degree or certification to retrieve discarded grocery store food. The dumpster... that is the place I started and I never wanted to be ashamed of that. After all, when you start at the bottom there is no place to go but up! Just be faithful where you are planted.

Serve God, your employers and your fellow man. Treat others like you would like them to treat you. That is the golden rule. Don't take yourself too seriously. People forget you quickly!

Study the Word, Pray and seek the Lord. He will guide you. Ask others to help, learn to reach out! Do not be ashamed or apologize for being blessed. Stay humble but thankful. God wants to enlarge the borders of your tent...increase not decrease...be the head not the tail. If you have been cast out or overlooked don't let that destroy your joy; they may have missed a great blessing...do not worry, your blessing is coming!

God is the one who first puts dreams in our hearts and minds. God qualifies those he has called even when they feel totally ill equipped. John 4:44 says a prophet is without honor in his own home town...There are always people around you who will say, 'go back, this will never work out for you.' They are full of negative talk and they love to throw cold water on your fire.

Hope deferred makes the heart sick. Your past hard struggles have led you to become the strong person you are right now. Do not fear. Stop telling God how bad everything is but give him praise and thanks.

Build others up, do not tear them down. It only makes you look bad. Rejoice when others do well. Stay true to your feelings. If they are not pure and loving deal with them quickly lest they become like a deadly disease. Most times it is better not to try and defend yourself and let others and God do it for you.

Within you is the same power that raised Jesus Christ from the dead. If he is with you, remember, who can be against you? Mother Teresa said, 'God has not called us to be successful, he called us to be faithful.' God never seems early but he is never late...my friend Bruce Huckins said, 'sometimes it seems like it takes God an awful long time to do something suddenly.'

Doubts and fears are dream killers, they obstruct miracles from taking place. God has chosen you for a special work and his hand is on you. He loves you so much. He will open doors when needed and close doors that need to be closed. Have the spirit that says, 'here I am Lord, send me.'

Sisters, we must remember to reach out to hurting people from all walks of life and every age group and meet their needs by being a listening ear, a shoulder to cry on, an arm to lean on, a helping hand and to assist women who would like to change their lives to become healthy, positive, and constructive members of our society, personally and professionally.

SCRIPTURE PROMISE

"Put on the whole armor of God, that ye may be able to stand against the wiles of the devil,"

— EPHESIANS 6:11

PRAYER

Dear Heavenly Father, thank you for calling all of us into full time ministry. You called it the great commission. I am so thankful you have given us the faith and the strength to continue in our ministry. I ask you now to show every woman and man reading this their gifts and bring clarity to their calling. Renew the vision once again. Stir up the gifts and anointing you have placed in each heart. We repent for our sins of all kinds and form. We choose willingly to give you our heart, body, soul and spirit right now in Jesus' name. Fill us with your Holy Spirit and your power. Amen.

8

SENIORS VIP

It was nearing year end and Peg Standish called and said, "Jackie, I want you to make a wish list. My husband Mike and I have a little extra money this year to donate. Make your list and think big. She and her husband Mike stopped by the ministry a few days after our conversation and presented me with a $25,000.00 check to Whosoever Will Outreach Ministries. Once a month we had special luncheons for senior women including music, food and inspirational speakers, usually myself, and trust me this luncheon was the highlight in most of their month. We had food distribution on Tuesday and Thursday at the Care Ministry so once a week our team would go to the nursing home just a couple of miles from the church. We would sing and hug and love on the people for about an hour and it was a very rewarding time for us all.

Peggy, a first-time volunteer, came to the food ministry and in the conversation I told her we visit the nursing home weekly and I had a nonprofit organization for hurting women. She wanted to come along and bring her children, which she did. I had by faith rented ministry offices but had no funds for furniture or supplies... but God made a way and because of that encounter at the nursing home our ministry offices and vehicle was provided.

Seniors, they all have great stories. They have done exploits, some working in high paying careers when they were young, but then perhaps the death or separation of a loved one and everything changed. I love their smiles. Their eyes sparkle when they laugh.

By the way, have you ever noticed how the roles change when you get older?

My daughter says, "Mom you are shuffling... you need to pick up your feet."

My son says, "Mom you are bending forward, you need to straighten up your back."

My conversations with myself seem to be increasing. If people walk up to me and I suddenly realize they are nearby I say, "oh my, you caught me singing...la la la." Also, my memory's not as sharp as it used to be. Every day should be precious for seniors. Surely there is some reward for surviving the struggles in life? I would advise anyone: if you plan on losing weight do it before 60. After that... well trust me; it is not pretty any way you look at it.

I have always made it a policy to keep my hair the same length and color. That way I can send out great pictures and when people see me in person they recognize me, even though they are probably thinking, how old was that picture? Sorry, it saves money and keeps me in the game. Hey there... it's really me!

You know, things just happen when you get older like…my eyes for instance; it took weeks before I realized I had this thing called floaters in my eye. I was continually swatting and trying to catch those little fluttery knats flying in front on my face. Funny, but after I discovered what it really was I hardly ever notice them!

Never look down into a mirror lest you might have a heart attack from the shock, and advise all grandchildren to seek permission before they post any picture of you on Facebook.

Remember to be nice…We cannot afford to make enemies or be a pain at this late stage in life.

Another time I decided to light Mother's cook stove but the pilot light went out. I lit the match, stuck it inside the oven and it blew me across the room…it was a good thing I had a wig and false eyelashes on because it matted them up in a ball!

I used to love to go to garage sales and we would go early, always with some excuse. One day I walked up to the door. The lady said, "come in." I noticed the little wooden divider doors, thinking it must be for a child and lo and behold two of the largest Great Dane dogs sailed over that fence and I almost broke my neck running backwards. Those dogs were like small horses.

Another time my daughter and I went to the door to ask the man if we could see the sale early. He said, "sure, my wife is not here. Come on in." He opened the door and had on his little tight underwear and again we walked backwards very fast…

And the time we saw a man going through all his fishing tackle and I started grabbing it, saying I want this and that. He stood there in shock. Finally I say, "you are having a garage sale?"

He says "No, I was just straightening out my garage." Come to find out we were on the wrong street.

Two old guys were sitting under a tree, watching the sun go down. One says, "You know, I'm 84 years old and my body is full of aches and pains. You're about my age, how do you feel?" The other guy says, "Oh, I feel like a newborn baby." Really," says the first guy."Yep," says the second one. "No teeth, no hair and I think I just wet my pants."

An elderly couple went to dinner at the home of some friends, also elderly. After dinner, the wives went into the kitchen and the two men were talking. One said, "We went out to dinner last night at a really good restaurant, I'd highly recommend it."

The second man said, "What's the name of it?" The first man thought and thought, then said, "What's the name of that flower you give to someone you love, the one that is usually red that has thorns?" "Oh, you mean a rose?" said the second man. "Yes, that's it," said the first man. Then he called to the kitchen, "Rose, what's the name of that restaurant we went to last night?"

SCRIPTURE PROMISE

And I saw the holy city, the new Jerusalem, descending out of heaven from God, all arrayed like a bride beautified and adorned for her husband;

— REVELATION 21:2

PRAYER

Dear Heavenly Father, thank you for giving the gift of eternal life. Thank you for giving us life and family. We praise your holy name and ask that our days will be fruitful and happy days. I bless my brothers and sisters in my family and my friends and ask that you continue to show mercy upon us all. Life is fragile. Help us to handle it with care. I love you and realize the older I get that every day and every breath is a gift from you. Help us to be especially caring to the elderly; they deserve respect honor and love. Amen.

9

ANOINTING A COSTLY GIFT

Seven handsome sons all lined up standing before the prophet. As he had passed them all by, he said, "Do you have any more sons?" … those guys were probably shocked! The father said, "One more, the youngest is David, who is in the field tending the sheep." The prophet said, "Go quickly and get him."

Can you imagine what David must have been thinking? Well, if he did not choose my brothers, why would he choose me? The prophet Samuel saw David, who was not the best looking, or most muscular, no, just a ruddy faced boy. Samuel knew immediately this young man would be anointed as king.

Saul was the first king that Israel had. God had chosen Israel as his own chosen people. The people insisted on having their own king and they chose Saul, a mighty man who was tall dark and handsome to be their King. At first he obeyed God but later was more concerned about pleasing people than he was about pleasing God…that is why God had sent the prophet Samuel to go to the house of Jesse who had eight sons.

One day David visited his brothers in the army and saw a huge giant named Goliath. No one was brave enough to go up against the giant...but David came forward and said to Saul, " I will go up against the giant." They laughed. "There is no way. He will kill you." David said, "The Lord has saved me from the mouth of lions and bears and I will kill the giant."

The giant laughed and roared, "You sent a boy to fight me; I will kill this boy", but David pulled back that sling and shot the rock right between his eyes where there was no armor and he fell over dead. David went over, grabbed the giant's sword and used it to cut off the head of the giant, then presented it to Saul.

Saul eventually lost his favor, which is the anointing of God. He became miserable and could not sleep but was tormented in his mind; so they sent for David who was an anointed harpist and sang beautiful psalms, which was all that quieted Saul's anxious heart.

Saul became jealous of David and wanted to kill him. Instead David honored Saul and loved him and refused to kill him even though he had the chance...but in due time, during a battle, Saul and his sons were killed and David, who had been anointed long before, took his rightful position as the King of Israel.

Some of you have known you were getting a certain position but you had to wait for what seemed like a very long time for it to come to pass. Remember, the key to success is hidden in your daily routine. Just bloom where you are planted.

Starting a food ministry from a dumpster did not make a lot of sense, but the natural mind does not understand the mind of Christ. Sometimes a calling, a vision, a dream does not make sense to others.

I was asked to choose between remaining on Pastoral staff at Restoration Church and having to give up Whosoever Will Outreach Ministries. Trust me, that was an easy but costly choice.

When I made the decision to step out in faith with Whosoever Will Outreach Ministries it happened at the same time I came to realize my mother needed my help and could no longer live alone. So even in that decision the Lord knew mother would take care of me and I would take care of my mother.

On January 8, 2003, I stepped out in faith and opened the new Whosoever Will Office in the offices of the International Fellowship building in Irving, Texas. The suite number was 101. A new beginning. I took the missions salary I was still getting from the church to set up and fund the offices of Whosoever Will.

One day, while all alone in my office, I locked the doors and for whatever reason felt so desperate, I was compelled to crawl under my big desk and get into the corner facing the wall. I cried out to God and he knew I felt so powerless and small. I said, "Lord, I have done my best to obey you and do everything with excellence, but this is too hard"…I cried and cried, then crawled back out and continued with my work. That was weird even to me.

I attended a meeting at Heartland Church and the founder of Hobby Lobby shared his testimony. He spoke of being a small business producing frames etc and that God put it in his heart to open the stores like he has now. He was so overwhelmed he shared how he was alone in his office and he too crawled into the corner under his desk and cried out to God!

Kathryn Kuhlman stated she believed God first called a man but he did not respond so he called her. I think God is looking for men and women who will say, "Here I am Lord, send me!"

Do not give up on your dreams and visions, in due season you will reap if you do not lose heart. Remain faithful, serve others and let the Lord close and open the doors that he wants open. Do not try to get ahead of God. You know he loves you, so do not try to make a position for yourself. The Lord raises up people and takes others down. Remember, you were anointed before the foundation of the world. God bless you, dear friend!

SCRIPTURE PROMISE

Now to him who is able to do exceedingly abundantly above all you can ask or think; according to the power that works within you.

— EPHESIANS 3:20

PRAYER

Dear Heavenly Father, thank you from the bottom of my heart for all my friends and family. You have blessed us with people who care. Help us to be gracious and never take one another for granted. Lord, I thank you for all the Pastors and Elders I have been privileged to serve under. I love them dearly. God bless them all. We are all seeking you. Now Father, you said if any person confesses with their mouth the Lord Jesus and believes in their heart that you, God, raised Jesus from the dead we will be saved. We believe, so help us all to hear and be faithful. Show us your way. Fill us with your Holy Spirit and power. Amen.

10

ATTITUDE

Smile and the world smiles with you. Cry and you cry alone. What we believe about our self and others is important in every aspect of life. If we think we are failures we will fail, if we think we are winners we will win, it is our choice. Every day we either choose life and happiness or gloom and despair. There will always be trouble in this life, hard times and seasons will come and go, but how we deal with those times and the attitude in our mind makes all the difference. When times are the hardest we must remember to deliberately have joy and keep a song in our heart.

Anytime we get our eyes on our circumstances and troubles it is easy to lose hope. When you feel this way the best solution is to begin thanking God for all he has done and who he is. It is like taking old dirty rags off and putting on the beautiful garments of praise and thanksgiving. They go together. Sadness and despair will not hang around a joyful happy heart.

My daughter worked for a company once who told their secretaries to keep a mirror by their phone. When the phone would ring they would look into the mirror and smile. They discovered it is almost impossible to sound rude when you are smiling! Think of it as putting on your happy face.

Paul said to know Christ and the power of his resurrection, the fellowship of his suffering, being conformed into his image... we must decrease, and he increases in every area of our life. I thank God for his compassion and love...he could have made it easy and left us to our own devices, but he did not because there is always a purpose in the pain.

I sense many of us were taken out of our comfort zones. It was hard, but we made it, and now we are stronger people because of that struggle. Seasons change and it is time to come out of your wilderness, and that means attitudes also must change! Yes, it was painful, but the Lord allowed those tests in our personal lives to grow us and mature our spiritual walk.

Perhaps you were wronged. I understand you may have been rejected and even discounted as an effective Christian. You might have lost your job and instead of a farewell parting and a gold watch you felt kicked to the curb. No matter what the testing, God is able to turn all those things that the devil meant for evil in your life...he meant to destroy you...but God will turn it for your good.

Look at Joseph's attitude... He who was rejected by his brothers, treated horribly...in due time Joseph was vindicated and the dreams he shared became a reality. He then became privileged to forgive his brothers and be a lifeline to his entire family as well as bless an entire nation. Joseph discovered it's almost impossible to have a bad attitude if you have a spirit of gratitude. That is why

Joseph could say to those who hurt him, "you meant this for evil, but God meant it for good."

You begin to wonder if God is even listening. Well he is, but his ways and timing are not like ours. He gives us the grace and strength to hold on and continue believing. May I encourage you. Do not give up. Victory may be the next prayer away. That is why we keep praying, because we believe nothing is too hard for him.

From time to time we need a reminder and a little attitude adjustment. It makes all the difference in the world. Speak it out loud right now, "I am a walking talking miracle, called, chosen, and set apart for such a time as this and my gifts will go before me and set me before kings and priests."

This is the way it works. There are times in life that are so dark and so sad you just want to pull the cover over your head and say, 'I can't do this, it is too hard' …but the Bible tells us weeping endures for the night but joy comes in the morning. This dark night of the soul will pass and there will soon be the dawn of a new day.

Forgive and forget past hurts whether you are right or wrong. One of these days that situation will turn around for good. Boundaries are good but walls are not…bridges let us cross back over to the other side; make sure you do not burn your bridges.

Just keep that wonderful happy attitude and people will be drawn to you like bees to honey. That smile of approval can break the ice of the coldest heart. You have so much to give, and so just get on with being your winning self; others will notice and be glad. Your God given gifts and your skills are surfacing. Be alert. People see your talents and your acts of kindness will win many hearts! May your attitude be one of gratitude from this day forward.

SCRIPTURE PROMISE

Enter into His gates with thanksgiving and a thank offering and into His courts with praise! Be thankful and say so to Him, bless and affectionately praise His name!

— PSALM 100:4

PRAYER

Dear Heavenly Father, thank you for loving us in spite of our faults and willful sins. Thank you for sending your son Jesus to pay the penalty for those sins. We confess Jesus is Lord and our Savior and with his own blood paid the full price for our salvation. He died and was resurrected and is now sitting at your right hand in Heaven. I admit boldly that God, Jesus and the Holy Spirit are a majority and all I need! I am so excited to proclaim I have an excellent attitude, because I know for certain you are pleased with me and are watching over me every step of my way. Amen.

11

BEAUTY TO ASHES

At the most fragile and vulnerable time of my life, I heard the devil speak clearly to my mind and say, 'I will give you everything you have ever dreamed of having, beauty, wealth and power. You will become famous and everyone will love and know you. All you have to do is say you love me and you will have it all!'

Of course, I wanted all those things. What young woman does not want love and acceptance?… But fear gripped my heart. What was he asking me to do…but sell my soul to the devil himself? Thank God I said "NO" and I meant every word!

Life used to seem so simple. I was born to loving Christian parents in a small East Texas town. Two sisters and a brother, they all knew hard times. Daddy worked from sun up till sun down share cropping and mother and my siblings worked in the fields. Mother faithfully canned all our food, stocking it up in a cellar for the hard months ahead.

As the youngest, I think in the midst of hard times I did not even know we were poor. My paper dolls were cut out of Sears catalogues and those pretty ladies took me to another place in time like Hollywood, movie stars and beautiful happy people. Now it seems like a lifetime past since being voted most beautiful in the sophomore class and later marrying the best looking basketball player in our small town.

Perched on the edge of my vanity stool looking into the mirror…I had an encounter with the devil. Still a 19 year old teenager I had just gotten a divorce from my high school sweetheart. We had two children born during that marriage. There had been much abuse and fighting and my heart was gripped with fear.

Looking back there was a divorce at 19, I remarried at 21 only married for a couple of months, and he almost beat me to death. The last time I saw him he was behind bars and said he'd get a gun…I believed him. I divorced him at 21and was married again at 23 to a country singer. One day he packed up and left me and I have never laid eyes on him since. So I was divorced again at 25. At 27 I married my last husband and we were married 15 years until he left me for a younger woman who was pregnant with his child.

God always has a plan, and at that vulnerable time in my life, rather than seek another husband, I sought the Lord. A beautiful ministry started. Even with my own broken life he gave me resources to help others who were broken, abused and needy. He birthed my ministry outreach.

I have remained single…I suppose because the Lord gave me something better, he gave me a calling on my life that would be far reaching and I would overcome my fears and the need of having a man in my life to fulfill me. I found that Jesus was enough and my past did not dictate my future! I discovered I had a destiny yet to be fulfilled.

The Bible says rebellion is as the sin of witchcraft. So sad that kids are running away to make it on their own only to find themselves working as sex slaves or prostitutes, trapped in addictive abusive lifestyles without hope and sensing no future. Countless nameless people murdered are unclaimed in big cities. 'God, help us reach these broken people before it is too late.'

Not long ago a Chaplain shared with me he had been in military service with a man who did great and heroic exploits. He was a war hero and given honors after arriving home. He was blessed to become a great successful leader and businessman and was highly esteemed, still good looking and full of charm.

Well, they lost touch for many years but one day he got a call from someone who shared that his friend was lying in a hospital dying with a terrible disease. He loved his old friend and he went to be by his side. The man recognized him and could still communicate.

The Chaplain said, "My friend, have you made your peace with God?" He responded, "I can't. Many years ago, I made a pact with the devil and I can never break it" ... The Chaplain said, "That is not right. Just ask Jesus in your heart. Ask him to forgive you for rejecting him." The man would not hear of it and said, "No... it is too late. I sold my soul to the devil"... The man died believing a devil's lie.

No matter where you have been or what you have done, even if you prayed to Satan, he cannot keep you from God's love and mercy. Renounce the devil right now. Say, 'Go, in Jesus' name.'

SCRIPTURE PROMISE

To grant to those who mourn in Zion—to give them an ornament of beauty instead of ashes, the oil of joy instead of mourning, the garment of praise instead of a heavy, burdened, and failing spirit—that they may be called oaks of righteousness the planting of the Lord, that He may be glorified.

— ISAIAH 61:3

PRAYER

Dear Heavenly Father, forgive me for being stubborn and willful and for doing my own thing. Right now I commit my life into your hands; I give you my heart, my dreams and my future. I am so sorry I have opened myself up and let demons come into my life. I turn my life over to you. I am sorry for hurting my family and for hurting myself. I ask you to set me free from every stronghold of sin and bondages, habits and addictions. I cast down and come against all spoken, prayed or promised curses over others and reject any alliance with the devil. I am a child of God and I will do my best to serve him. Forgive me for hurting others; help me to be of service to you and my fellow man. Fill me with your Holy Spirit, I pray! I take my authority and I resist the devil, he must flee from me! Amen.

12

DEATH TO LIFE

I held my dear Mother in my arms and remembered her telling me, "I keep dreaming I hear you calling me, saying 'get up Mother, get up Mother.'" I remembered jokingly saying, "Well you need to dream something else because you might jump out of bed real quick and fall." But this was no joke; Mother had cardiac arrest while sitting across from me at the breakfast table. I thought, 'now Lord, what do I do? He said, "There is no time to call for help. You must help her."

Ecclesiastes says to everything there is a season. On an ordinary Friday we sure had some excitement here and as it turned out, it was a life changing Friday for me and my mother... That morning we got up the unusual time and I fixed Mother's coffee and cereal, and her favorite blueberry waffles. We were at the table and normally I take my coffee and go check my email or turn on the news and see what happened in the night, but Mother liked to just sit at the breakfast table and read the newspaper. I stayed seated at the table... I was sick of the news, so I too was looking through the paper with Mother.

Suddenly she said, "Oh!". She was holding her upper part of her stomach under the heart. The pain seemed to pass and I looked down, momentarily, then heard another gasping sound, looked back up and Mother was sitting up, her head totally back and mouth wide open and eyes in a fixed stare. No breath, no sound, no life!

With or without training, you never really know what you will do in this kind of situation, but I do know this...I heard the Lord say there is no time to call 911. You must take care of her yourself.

I began working on her myself. She was frail. I did not want to break any ribs, so I held her close and pressed my left hand on her chest and began pounding up and down her back. Her body felt rigid.

She had told me several times, in the weeks before, she had dreamed very clearly that I was calling her name and saying, "Get up Mother... get up" ...over and over again. The Lord reminded me of those dreams, so that is what I did at the same time as pounding her back, careful not to break any ribs. I was yelling, "Mother, get up... Mother, get up!" I said, "You are not going to die...no... Mother, get up." Well, the Lord was gracious and it seemed like several minutes but she began to breathe again. She had lost all bodily functions and was gone for what seemed like a lifetime.

When she started to breathe, I called 911 and then they came and took her to the hospital emergency. Her heart beat was very faint...so she had a pacemaker put in on Monday afternoon. Dr. Pitts, Mother's primary care doctor said, "Well, Mrs. Jackson you were dead, but your daughter brought you back."

I thank God for those extra months we had with her. God uses ordinary people to do exploits throughout life. I truly believed when he said you shall lay hands on the sick, and they will recover, cast out demons and do many wonderful works, it can happen. I feel we are all given faith and gifts to be used as the needs arrive.

Mother loved the Lord and had no fear of Hell but had always been fearful of actually dying. She said she had no idea how very peaceful it was to have the lights go out and then come back on so brightly, especially when she said, "Lord, I do not want to die today." I asked her more than once, "Mother did you see a tunnel?" She said, "No, the lights just started to go out, no fear."

I was Care Ministry Pastor at Restoration Church in Euless Texas for 15 years, and mostly volunteers manned it. One day Bill Pierson's son dropped him off and as he walked in he said, "I dreamed about you last night and you were my angel." I told him, "Well, that is wonderful." As usual we hugged, and he went on back to the pantry with the other volunteers. Shortly after, someone called out for help shouting, "We are losing Mr. Bill."

I rushed back to the pantry and out of my inner being I began saying, forcefully, "You are not going to die. You are going to live." I heard a faint little sneeze. Not knowing if that was life leaving his body, I said again, "No, you will not die, we are here, you will live, we all love you". He sneezed two times. The volunteers were standing in the doorways stunned and probably thinking I had lost my mind but when they heard the two sneezes they too began saying we love Mr. Bill. He sneezed three times then…he opened his eyes and within minutes was sitting up and drinking orange juice.

I quietly disappeared and went into the bathroom. My legs were as feeble as a wet noodle; I began shaking all over, with the realization of what just happened. Mark 5:25-34 tells us of when Jesus and his disciples were walking through a huge crowd. A woman who had been sick for years thought, 'if I can just touch the hem of his garment I will be healed.' She touched him, and he turned and said, "who touched me?"

The disciples said, "How can we know who touched you, Lord, with all these people around?" Jesus said, "Someone touched me, for I felt virtue leave my body." Still shaken, I made my way to the break room and found a slice of bologna in the refrigerator and ate it just to steady myself. I was elated. What a glorious experience.

It was all so incredible we did not even speak of it; yet Mr. Bill lived to be almost 104 years old and I was privileged to perform his going home funeral service. He died from complications after a surgery with pneumonia, not old age. Why do we doubt these stories when Jesus said we would see and do greater miracles?

SCRIPTURE PROMISE

Jesus said, "I am the resurrection and the life, He who believes in me will live, even though he dies, and whosoever believes in me will never die."

— JOHN 11:25

PRAYER

Dear Lord Jesus, thank you so much for your tender love and care. Thank you for the time we have been given. Help us to use it wisely and not live with regrets. Thank you for opportunities to change some situations that either we were powerless or too stubborn to change ourself. Open our eyes and our hearts to the needs of those who are fragile and broken, poor or alone, and give us tender hearts to reach out and be a helping hand. Lead us in the way you would have us go and show us the light at the end, because you are our guiding light. Amen.

13

PRUNED WITH A PURPOSE

The new Pastor walked into my office at the beginning of the New Year … He said, "Jackie, I believe God gave me a word for you." My eyes opened wide and ears perked up ready to hear a great prophetic word, envisioning him saying what a fabulous work I was doing and it had not gone unnoticed.

Many thoughts popped into my mind, perhaps a raise or bonus. I thought, 'Thank God someone has finally seen my heart and I am celebrated and will not simply feel tolerated.' I smiled and tears came into my eyes, tears of joy and feeling great love.

He said, "Jackie, you are going to be severely pruned! It will be very painful, but it is the Lord and it will work out well for you one day." Duh, like I want to hear that. How much better to have a word like, "you are going to get blessed beyond measure, more than you could dream"… or at least just have said nothing. Even my own mother always said if you can't say something nice then say nothing at all.

I told Susan, my assistant, I think my job is being cut. Susan said, "surely not? Why would you even think a thing like that?" Well, because he had said you do such a great work; your ministry is like a well-oiled machine, in fact it's so smooth they don't even need you there. I know you have your ministry; you could be traveling and ministering to women around the world.

He went on to say very kind words regarding my ministry gifting. I admit his words became muffled in the cloud of fear now enveloped into 'now what?' questions. If I knew anything about my gifting, I knew it was just common sense anointing for discernment and seeing deeper than mere words spoken. It is a gift from God and has carried me through many hard tests in my life.

Sure enough, a few months passed and I was called in and given the choice to give up my non-profit organization or step down from my Care Ministry Pastoral Staff paid position at the Church, one or the other. I couldn't do both. They also said the ministry was going to be changed into another format and I would be coordinating it. Oh, my goodness, this is hard, 15 years, my only ministry work experience.

The Lord had put me right in the middle of a rapidly growing Charismatic Church with six seasoned Elders and Staff Pastors. I tell you, when I sat in that conference room at the table with all those mighty men and women I had to pinch myself, it seemed too good to be true.

I had always felt so fortunate to be on the staff with them. I got paid so well and was very grateful, believe it or not. I thought to myself, 'I wish I could just live and walk by faith and not have to take a salary.'

I sensed in my heart the Lord say, "You can do both", but I kept it to myself so I could be sure before responding. I knew that meant no salary, no job, no location! After all, the Care Ministry was my baby, birthed out of loss and pain. Come to think of it, that is how birth is, painful.

I prayed and waited a couple of months to give my final answer which was, the Lord says I can do both. They responded, "ok" but not here, so I was given one year's salary and a promise to be on the missions after that time. They asked me to continue until the end of the year – until after the Care Ministry Christmas Party.

One of the Elders asked, "Jackie, do you believe we all hear God?" I said, "Yes I do." He said, "Well, why do you think he would tell us no and you yes?"… My answer, "I know you all hear God and I do not know why he is telling you one thing and me something else."

Oh, dear Lord, I can only say I was grieved at that decision even though I knew it was God. I felt like a mother over the loss of her child. I knew firsthand how that felt inside my heart because of losing my first-born son, Mike, at 27 years of age. For me having birthed children and a ministry did not feel all that different at the time of loss.

We pray for open and closed doors…and many times we are called to make hard decisions so crucial that it literally changes the course of our life. It is like you are pulled from the frying pan and thrown into the fire of affliction…sometimes we just don't get it. We feel punished for doing what we believed to be right.

Pruning… no, we do not enjoy being pruned. Try to remember it is God who is cutting off old needless lifeless branches, clipping off those showy flowers. We had probably gotten a bit proud. Pruning is painful. You may even wonder and hope that there is something good enough inside to remain after the severity of pruning.

Seasons change, thank God, and with prayer requests and thanksgiving to him, crying many tears which are good for watering some fertilizer, which is the Word of God hidden deep within our hearts for growth, we find ourselves coming out and can sense the buds and leaves beginning to form. In this we find new hope, new life, new promise and new futures.

Gethsemane is the Hebrew word for crushing olives... being pruned and purified, and like the olives, the pruning for us results in dying to self and gaining true mature anointing that God desires to come forth in our life and calling.

Do not cry over the past, but look ahead. Do not forget he is the light of the world and you, my friend, are like a city set on a hill. So let that light shine. His death, burial and resurrection on your behalf and your own pruning has made it all possible for you to shine! Rejoice and be glad.

SCRIPTURE PROMISE

The upright (honorable, intrinsically good) man out of the good treasure [stored] in his heart produces what is upright (honorable and intrinsically good), and the evil man out of the evil storehouse brings forth that which is depraved (wicked and intrinsically evil); for out of the abundance (overflow) of the heart his mouth speaks.

— LUKE 6:45

PRAYER

Dear Heavenly Father, I thank you right now for reminding me of your deep and unchangeable love you have for me. Even though things happen I might not understand or even explain, my heart's desire is to say yes to you and not question your love. Even in those times of feeling I am in a pit, help me remember you have given me hope and vision for the future. I continually need your help to stay out of the pit. Hope deferred makes the heart sick so I rebuke the spirit of hopelessness and pray for courage and strength, knowing that remaining in you I will be strong and do exploits. Thank you right now for renewed hope, vision, dreams and fresh anointing. My life is in your hands because I put my trust in you. Amen.

A FOOLISH THING

Flies and gnats swarmed aimlessly around the open dumpster that sweltering Father's Day. Little did I know I was walking into my destiny being birthed from the Father's heart. God would use my young son Howard and his friend to help redirect my uncertain future. I asked, "Where did you get those grapes Howard? He answered, "That new specialty store is throwing boxes of fruits and vegetables in the dumpster."

I reached into the shiny new green dumpster to pull out a precariously stacked box of purple grapes stacked on boxes of apples and oranges; I was almost overcome with excitement. I set the box of grapes on the ground next to me and bent into the dumpster again to get a better look. Wow! I could see all kinds of produce, beautiful fresh produce, just discarded, stacked haphazardly in corrugated boxes.

I strained to pull out every box I could reach without falling in myself. This was, for me, a simple act of obedience to the Holy Spirit's prompting. I later came to realize, God was inaugurating his call on my life to minister to him by ministering to the poor, the needy and the hurting. I believe God raised up a banner that day to assemble the out-casts, the wounded and broken people who would be drawn to what became known as the Care Ministry.

After retrieving this treasure trove I felt prompted to take them to an apartment complex located just behind my home church. I silently prayed for wisdom and direction as I drove into the parking lot and immediately noticed a young woman and a few little children huddled against her thin arms and legs.

I got out of my car and approached the woman with a greeting, "Hello, would you like some fruit and vegetables?" She said, "I don't have any money." I replied, "You don't need money, It's free…. from the Lord".

She replied, "I just fed my children the last of our food this morning. I told them there was nothing left to eat." Well, before you know it, the young mother and I were crying, hugging and laughing as her children danced about, giggling and stuffing bananas into their already stuffed mouths.

Meeting this woman's desperate need that day exhilarated me and penetrated every bone in my body. Just like the woman who fed Elijah her last little bit of oil and flour, the supply of fruits and vegetables to the ministry never ran out. In fact, the more we gave away, the more the Lord provided for us to give.

Who would have thought a ministry would begin in a dumpster, but then who would have believed a king would be born in a stable? So many times we assume every great work started with a dream, a plan and a strategy.

The Lord, in his mercy and by his grace, did something for me that was no less than a miracle. He took a broken woman not all that different from the woman he met at a well (John 4) and turned my life in a totally different direction. For that woman who was a Samaritan living with a man and had been married five times, she too never dreamt that she would encounter the man who would change her life, her direction, her focus and her call.

For her, after she discovered the man Jesus knew everything about her and yet she felt his forgiveness and love, she got so excited she actually ran back to the city and told everyone, "Come, see a man who knows everything about me. He is the Messiah." Because of that woman's divine appointment with destiny not only was her life changed but also a city and so much more.

Many lives were changed and for 13 years twice weekly I saw one, if not more, accept Jesus as their Savior on those special days. Drug addicts delivered to this very day, some called into ministry, but all touched by the simple love of Jesus Christ in a very practical way. I always had a thought maybe a Billy Graham would be raised up out of that very place.

Emmaus Road Ministry School was there on the campus and I always secretly wished I could attend. One day I mentioned it to one of the teachers. He said, "Jackie, you are doing the stuff we teach. You are also helping those students while they are making sacrifices of that year of training to endure their hardships by providing groceries." I got it… some sow, some water but God gets the glory!

If you are sensing God is calling you into missions or the ministry I might suggest start by volunteering with a Church or group and let God open the doors for you. Please do not use your natural gifts to make things happen quickly; too many times that does not work.

If you want the blessing and the anointing, first serve and observe others and God will bless the work of your hands. I have heard it is good to be a Christian and know it, but better to be a Christian and show it!

God sometimes uses foolish things to confound the wise. He has shown me I was indeed a foolish thing, which was a good thing for me, because he was well pleased. The Bible says he sits in the Heavens and laughs...you and I are adorable to him. He finds pleasure in us.

SCRIPTURE PROMISE

And he replied, 'you must love the Lord your God with all your heart and with all your soul and with all your strength and with all your mind; and your neighbor as yourself.'

— LUKE 10:27

PRAYER

Dear Heavenly Father, thank you for the privilege of serving our fellow man. Give us eyes to see the needs, ears to hear their cries and a heart of compassion to serve. You said people would know our love for you because of our love for others. Thank you for loving the world so much you sent your only son into the world to seek and to save the lost. Come into my heart, Lord Jesus. Fill me with your Holy Spirit, I pray. Amen.

15

A TEXAS TALE

In the summer of 1923, my Grandfather had been witness to a murder. Justice required him to testify in a court against the murderer. One summer night before the trial, a lone man on horseback rode up to his house, called him out, and in front of my Grandmother and the children, shot him through the chest while still sitting on his horse. My Granddaddy bled and died right there on the front porch as they stood there watching; now a family, even generations later, are changed forever by that violent act of murder.

That poor little girl became my mother, who forever had that memory etched in her mind witnessing her Daddy being shot down in cold blood. The "tragedy" is now a page of our family history, a brutal reminder of the lawless Texas territory, back when Texas seemed like a land of oil entrepreneurs, renegades, pioneers and missionaries. Mother and her little brother Jack were raised by our Grandmother (Big Mama) and Papa Colvin.

The horror of something like this can turn some people away from God forever. But not my grandmother. She was so strong and determined to raise her children in the church.

Mother said her family owned land, so they were raised on the farm and farmed, girls and women, and worked just like any man would do. She remained single and worked very hard all her life and sacrificed much to care for her children.

Mother was fifteen when she married Daddy. He was twenty-one. They both had similar backgrounds coming from northeast Texas *farming* families. One Sunday, a year or so before I was born, the Lord called Daddy into an instant conversion, and from that day on he never touched another drop of liquor.

By the time I was born, my parents had two girls, Barbara and Marita, and a boy, Don. My mother hoped for a second son, and she already had picked out a name. He'd be named Jack Jackson, after Jackie's uncle Jack, Mother's little brother who was stationed in Burma fighting in the war.

Daddy remembered it well. Mother asked him from the hospital bed, "Sorry, but is it a little girl?" Daddy said, "I thank God she's a little girl", and the Lord began to speak to him there in that hospital room, and he repeated what he heard. "One day this little girl will do God's work and sing praises to His name."

Mother and Daddy liked the preaching in the Baptist church, and the Spirit inside the Pentecostal church. Driving home, Mother and Daddy would discuss the sermon to themselves while we listened in the back seat. We kids always felt good when they talked the sermon over together. It was so reassuring.

To crown the main event of Church each Sunday, we always invited the Pastor over to eat dinner with us whenever he could make it. We took more than our turn at feeding the pastor. Mother could really cook, and this was a special day. The family was really in for something when the pastor came by.

My sisters Barbara and Marita were very pretty and talented. Daddy always said they were the most beautiful girls in Avery. They would be bustling all over that kitchen like they each had a special boy coming over. There was almost more food than the table could hold. It seemed that we had six kinds of desserts to choose from. The pastor would say, "Lord, I think I've eaten so much I'm sure I won't be able to preach tonight." When he left, Daddy would say, "I don't recall anyone twisting his arm to eat that much", and we would all laugh happily at that remark.

At last a visit from Uncle Jack, Mother's brother, who was quite a man in my eyes. He was the hero of the family, having been a decorated medic in World War II. He served in both the Army and Marines. Remember, I was named after him, something I was reminded of often, and he was tall and handsome. I always wanted Uncle Jack to like me.

One night Uncle Jack brought over a woman named Flo for a visit. They were in the other room and all of a sudden we heard this big commotion. We ran in and Uncle Jack was just beating up this woman, to the point were Daddy had to kick him out. She had black eyes for a week after and it was really a bad scene.

That scared me and everybody else, too. I don't know why he did something like that. I think it had to do with his drinking and that the Lord wasn't in his life. After he kicked him out, Daddy said any man who hit a woman was a coward. Who would ever imagine that someday I would become a woman like Flo with black eyes, bruises and a broken spirit? Thank God, he can heal the broken and bruised hearts of hurting people.

I have heard you can pick your friends but you can not pick your family. God knew what he was doing when he placed us in a family. It may have been a great happy experience for you or it might have been horrible. In either case we deal with the hand we have been given. We choose to love, and forgive. My family members are all very independent people who care deeply for their families. At a time of need or crisis they are there for one another. That is a good family to me.

SCRIPTURE PROMISE

My son, (daughter) attend to my words; incline your ear to my sayings. Let them not depart from your eyes; keep them in the midst of your heart. For they are life to those that find them, and health to all their flesh.

— PROVERBS 4:20-22

PRAYER

Dear Heavenly Father, thank you so much for allowing me to be born into a Christian family. Many who are praying with me right now were not that blessed. Father, please show each one how much you truly accept and love them. You are so precious in his sight. Lord, you said you would be a Father to the fatherless. Only you can fill those empty places in the hearts of your children who missed that from their earthly father growing up. You are our hope and in you do we place our hopes, dreams and our trust. You have our heart. We love you Jesus. Amen.

16

CANCER DOES NOT DEFINE YOU!

"Sorry Jackie, but you have stage four Chronic Lymphocytic Leukemia." The Oncologist said, "Get your house in order and live your life; try not to worry, and call if you need us. The good news is I think it is slow growing." However, he said calmly, "If you have night sweats, fever, weight loss, extreme tiredness, rashes, nose bleeds, then we can give some treatments." Excuse me. Did I just hear what I think he said? You not only have cancer but it is terminal and you are going to die! Well, alright then… I had all but two so I toughed it out with the help of getting my nose packed with that awful tube hanging out of my nose taped to my face, steroids and antibiotics, plus allergic burns from iodine after CAT scans. Not to mention stress related shingles. I think you see the picture!

Still wanting to please my mother, on October 16, 2013 I decided to rush into Walgreens and get my flu shot. I believe he gave me the one for people over 65, which I was at the time. I went in feeling great but that shot caused my immune system to go haywire. Every year I had taken the flu shot and there was no reaction before but this time within three days my arm was red and swollen, aching and itching almost to the bone; but mainly I felt horrible like flu. I made an appointment with my doctor and got antibiotics and within a few days I went to the ER for a shot and more medication.

By the first of November I noticed an size lymph node swollen under my left arm, the next day lymph nodes erupted on the left side of my neck. The next day one on the right and when I called the doctor said, "Keep taking antibiotics; it was probably an infection and would go away." My doctor sent me to an Oncologist who said, before any tests were even made, "If I were guessing I would say you have indications of lymphoma."

He made an appointment with a surgeon for me to have a lymph node removed to be checked. I was in day surgery. They put me to sleep and took out the lymph node to check to see the problem. He said, "It looks like lymphoma", but after a couple of weeks decided to do a bone marrow biopsy.

The day of my diagnosis… was on a cold January day in 2014. Charlsey had driven down from Tennessee to spend some time with me and to be here when her first grandbaby was born. While pulling into the hospital parking lot Isaiah, my grandson called and said the baby is coming, hurry.

The phone rang. It was the Oncologist himself calling to give us the results of my bone marrow tests. He said, "I have your reports and wanted to give you the results."

I put the speaker phone on so Charlsey could hear also. He said it was cancer and we will need to have you come in to the office and we can discuss the options for treatment.

God's timing is perfect. The atmosphere in the Hospital waiting room was spirited and happy, all sides of the family waiting to see that beautiful new baby girl, Scarlett! God knew it would be a good time for us to get the results. The last thing I wanted to do was cause alarm to anyone, especially my grandson, at this happy moment. (I am now a great grandmother of Scarlett and Bearon.)

My daughter Charlsey and son Howard sat with me across from the Oncologist in his office. I asked what stage it was in… expecting maybe stage 1 or 2 but he said "stage 4." My kids and I looked at each other in shock and then at him. I say, "Isn't that the highest?" He said, "Yes it has spread but it is slow growing!" My children broke down and cried like babies. I think I was in shock; I was thinking, "Wow, they love me so much and they think I am dying." I assured them I would be fine. God will take care of me.

I did not want to take any treatments. I did not feel strong enough to go through all that. I would just take my chances. He thought that was a good idea. If I got real sick they could do other treatments. He said for this type of cancer less is more since it is in the blood marrow and cells. So why have side effects from other drugs?

*Shocked yes…*but I sensed strongly God speaking to me and said, "You shall live and not die but declare the works of the Lord." A time later he put in my heart, 'Your healing is in water, drink lots of water.'

I decided to go with prayers and continue my work and eat more vegetables and drink more water! The Lord always provides. One day I was at the store working and I shared with a new customer,

Judy McCarley, about what the Lord had said about the water. She ran to her car, brought in cases of H9Water, then later antioxidant seeds and products called Soul and Core which are seeds from Rain International and provided them for me.

My friend Susan Reddick, a nurse, did research and said take the Zyrtec for the allergies, that is the best remedy for the rashes from your type of cancer. My daughter Charlsey sent me several bottles of Turmeric as she felt the Lord said that will kill the cancer.

What is Chronic Lymphocytic Leukemia? Cancer starts when cells in the body begin to grow out of control. Cells in nearly any part of the body can become cancer, and can spread to other areas of the body. Chronic Lymphocytic Leukemia (CLL) is a type of cancer that starts from cells that become certain white blood cells (called *lymphocytes*) in the bone marrow. The cancer (leukemia) cells start in the bone marrow but then go into the blood.

God is bigger than CANCER or any other disease. Have faith in the fact he promised to never leave you or forsake you. Hold those you love close to your heart, love passionately, laugh boldly. Enjoy some of those one day dreams or vacations. Share those dreams with others and do not be surprised that dreams do come true after all.

SCRIPTURE PROMISE

Why are you cast down, O my inner self? And why should you moan over me and be disquieted within me? Hope in God and wait expectantly for Him, for I shall yet praise Him, my Help and my God.

— PSALM 42:5

PRAYER

Dear Heavenly Father, thank you for giving me breath and hope for eternal life. Thank you for being with me and promising that you are my healer. I pray for healing for myself, my friends and loved ones; I will do my best to place my trust in you. Thank you, Jesus, for salvation and as part of your suffering you understand our needs and by your own stripes we are healed. Thank you for never leaving or forsaking us. Thank you, Holy Spirit, for guiding our way. Bless our doctors, nurses and most of all our families and friends. Let me be a faithful witness in this thing called life. Amen.

17

HAVE YOU TRIED MY SERVANT JACKIE?

I felt relief, my youngest son was alive but I asked the Lord, "I still don't understand why this happened to Howard." He definitely had got my attention; he told me in my spirit, "I broke his leg and I am carrying him." I broke down right there next to my son in that hospital room and wept. It was quite a picture. My son groaning in pain, and me weeping and crying, saying "Thank you, Jesus."

I remembered reading how a shepherd would discipline a sheep that was jumping out of the pen to wander astray. To train the sheep to quit wandering, the shepherd would break one of his legs and then carry the little sheep on his shoulders wrapped around his neck until his leg healed. The shepherd would speak tenderly to the little sheep and gently caress it as he carried him about. The little lamb learned obedience in the suffering. He also learned the tenderness of the shepherd and that he could trust the shepherd.

Early October 1989, I was at a women's prayer meeting. In prayer, I heard the Lord speaking to the devil, "Have you tried my servant, Jackie?" I thought to myself, "Who do I think I am to suppose that God is equating me to Job?" Again, I heard it. I heard that voice in a matter-of-fact way say, "Have you tried my servant, Jackie?" Immediately, faith rose up in my spirit and said, "Yes, Lord, whatever you want me to do."

Matthew 20:22, Jesus asked his disciples, "Are you able to drink the cup that I am about to drink?" Many turned away from Jesus, because his words were too hard for them. The Lord spoke to my heart, "Are you willing to sell all your goods to feed the poor?" "Yes, Lord, I am willing." I remember that seemed like such a joy to finally have such a stubborn selfish heart say yes and mean it completely. Saying yes may cost you everything but, trust me, he is worth it. Just keep in mind, there is always a purpose in the pain.

Sensing something different than I had ever felt before, I leaned over and shared this with Betty Godwin, one of the leaders in the group. She quickly said, "We need to pray for Jackie" then she shared with them what the Lord had just said.

About a week after that, I came home from the Care Ministry and noticed the red light flashing on my answering machine. I was shocked to hear a message from the Police Department, a man's authoritative voice saying, "Call us immediately. Your son has been in an accident. He has been hit by a car."

Shaking, terrified, I returned the call. I discovered that my youngest son, Howard, 15, had been rushed to the emergency room of a local hospital in excruciating pain with his leg broken in several places. He had been struck by a car while riding his moped, ironically enough, not more than 10 feet from where he had picked up the first bunch of grapes, which it turns out, birthed The Care Ministry. They put his leg in traction and kept him sedated with morphine until it could be set two days later.

Years later, Howard confided to me that he and his friends had already made plans to ride their mopeds on Airport Freeway to Dallas that night to party with some friends and, in fact, they had done this before.

Three weeks after Howard came home from the hospital, I arrived home one chilly November evening and found Mike dead in the backyard. **The day part of me died**… November 16, 1989, a cold November day, Mike decided to stay home from work. That night I lost my prayer partner, my first-born child, my son and my trusted friend. My son Michael David Phelps age 27 made his decision and took his life.

Mike loved the Lord and I had been praying against the suffering he had physically in his feet and nerves in his legs. Mike was born with Cerebral Palsy and the older he got the more pain he suffered with leg and feet cramps. He was experiencing a lot of depression. I prayed for healing and I prayed that he would be at peace in his heart.

He was very lonely and talked of seeing Jesus. I just had no way of knowing it would be the way he went, quickly peacefully. Once he had made up his mind he was gone, only 27 years of age. I sensed the Lord say, 'Do not be afraid. Mike is with me.' I never doubted that a moment!

Everyone has trials and troubles. If you live very long at all you see that everyone suffers in some way during their lifetime. There is a by product of suffering…you grow stronger if you are a believer. No one likes to hurt but tribulation works patience and patience gives hope and hope gives us confidence and we have no shame.

Remember the story of Job? It is said to be the oldest book in the Bible. A man the Bible said loved God and hated evil. He was a great leader and well respected in the community. In fact he was the greatest man in all the earth at that time.

He was blessed in every way...but in only a few days everything changed for Job. God allowed Satan to test his life, destroy his flock, kill his children and destroy his health. God said, 'You cannot kill him.' His oxen and camels were stolen, his sheep died; a tornado destroyed his home, his children and their spouses. His health failed, his wife turned against him and even commented, 'Why don't you curse God and die?'

A few of his friends tried to encourage him but eventually tired of it and they began to accuse him of sinning. He was sick, had sores and infection all over his body. But Job's captivity and life turned around when he prayed for his friends. Sometimes suffering seems to wear others down. We all have different tests and trials. I shared these two of mine and the story of Job to say good times, bad times, struggles in life can happen to anyone. You are not being punished.

God is in control and like Job we must say at the end of our days...if he slays me yet will I trust him. Many things happen in life. We simply do not understand but we trust that God is in total control and what the devil means for evil, God will turn for our good.

SCRIPTURE PROMISE

Humble yourselves [feeling very insignificant] in the presence of the Lord, and He will exalt you.

— JAMES 4:1

PRAYER

Dear Heavenly Father, I thank you that you know my heart, you hear my prayers and you know my needs. Father, sometimes I forget how great you are and right now I acknowledge you as creator and God of the Universe. No matter what may come or go in my future I will hold on to your unchanging hand. Thank you for loving me. I am yours forever. I say yes to you, dear Lord. Amen.

18

HEALER BODY SOUL AND SPIRIT

Someone said they could not bear to hear another person say, "God just needed another angel" ... The person who lost their loved one may be thinking, "Well, why did he not take yours?" Truthfully, a person just doesn't know how they will feel with loss and bereavement, unless they too have experienced it first hand and even then each is unique and deals with it in a very real and personal way. When attempting to bring comfort most of the time helping and comforting is bearing another's burdens, meeting their needs, weeping with them and showing your love by simply being nearby or a phone call away. God is with us in the valley of the shadow of death. He said we would fear no evil.

Adam and Eve, by their fall, brought sin into the world. Their disobedience brought disease and death. Sin is the work of the devil and Jesus was manifested to destroy the works of the devil. The devil came to steal, kill and destroy but Jesus came to bring life.

In one seed there is a potential tree a million times bigger than the seed itself. All God's wonders are in the seed and God can accomplish things greater than we can imagine. A single seed...the gospel seed planted in good fertile soil can bring forth a harvest of blessings.

Death comes to all! After Jesus died his imperishable seed needs to be planted in the hearts of man, then continually watered and cultivated. The incorruptible seed is the Word of God. We are on a journey, all traveling down different directions, forks and turns in the road.

The Book of Acts is showing how ordinary people do the stuff: such as praying for the sick and seeing them recover, bringing sight to the blind, setting captives free, raising the dead, and seeing with our eyes signs, wonders and miracles. The Word of God is to be honored. The Word is the seed...the seed of faith must be planted in hearts in order for people to believe and receive their healing.

We pray for healing. As long as there is breath there is hope! Believing God's words and promises are crucial. The prayer of faith heals the sick.

Proverbs 4: 20-22:

Attend to my words incline your ear unto my sayings. Let them not depart from thine eyes; keep them in the midst of thine heart. For they are life unto those that find them, and health to all their flesh.

Hebrews 11:1:

Faith is the substance of things hoped for and the evidence of things not seen.

The enemy wants to plant seeds of doubt and fear...weeds choking out your faith. Doubt your doubts, but don't doubt your faith. Believe your prayers are being answered.

JEHOVAH-RAPHA means I am the Lord thy Physician or I am the Lord who healeth thee! The Holy Spirit lives inside the believer and the same power that raised Jesus from the dead lives inside us. Some people even get healed taking communion or the anointing with oil or the laying on of hands by the elders and faithful believers. Faith has expectation. If you do not believe, you are double minded.

The Holy Spirit says in the face of every need confess boldly that the Lord is your Shepherd and you shall not want. We are the Lord's garden. Let the Word grow in you.

Hide it in your heart.

Phil. 4:8:

Whatsoever things are true, pure lovely, of good report then think on these things.

Speaking words of faith and life over a sick or hurting person can be powerful when spoken with true sincerity, compassion and love.

Healing is for today, but not all are healed. All will eventually die and then those left behind have no choice but to deal with it, whether they are ready to let them go or not. This is a fact. You can have the best Christian doctors and medicine and see the patient lose their battle. The richest and the poorest have one thing in common when the death angel knocks on their door... the Lord is the maker of them all. Money or power is totally of no value when that day comes.

Death rewrites the script of your life...it is not a bump in the road, but the road is gone and you must take your life in a different direction...all done without your permission. Once in a church service after Mike's death my heart just broke and I began to weep. I remember a minister came close to me not to embrace me but to calm me down so I did not bring disorder. It was not a good time but I could not help myself. The reality of him being gone swept over me like a dark cloud and for a couple of minutes I was like Rachel in the Bible, weeping for my child and I could not be comforted.

God is the only one that can bind up and heal wounded broken hearts...but a broken spirit is impossible to heal unless you deal with the loss, not rehash old mistakes. When they are gone that is impossible. Is everyone healed? No, not on this earth, but we continue to pray and believe for healing.

It is so important to have friends, loved ones or counselors to help direct your way out of despair and hopelessness. Life goes on. People around you laugh and you want to scream...that person whether young or old, good or bad, was so irreplaceable. To me the best counsel is to offer God's hope and remind the grieving person that the Holy Spirit is the Comforter and the next best advice is to listen to their stories over and over again if need be.

The best words I ever heard shared were from a lady who said, "Your son sounds so wonderful. I only wish I had known him"...now that was Jesus with flesh!

SCRIPTURE PROMISE

"If I had cherished sin in my heart, the Lord would not have listened; but God has surely listened and has heard my prayer".

— PSALM 66:18-19

PRAYER

Dear God, I surrender my will to become your will. No longer do I want to serve myself but I want very much to bring glory and honor to you. Strengthen me by the power of your might. Guide me with your eye. Show me the way to go. You said to follow you and we would never be ashamed. Thank you for loving us in spite of our self and sending your son Jesus to show us the way... Thank you for determining to make us beautiful not broken, not ugly but precious and reflecting your light. Thank you for the good times and yes, even the bad. We know you are our healer and yet you help us in our times of grief. Bring back the joy to the one reading this right now, I pray. Amen.

19

LET ME ENTERTAIN YOU

"You are the most beautiful woman here. You just need the right man who will treat you right." You hear all the stories. Some are true, most one sided and untrue. You tell yourself it is my body to do with what I want, and think of all the money you will make. You want to believe it; oh, you want to believe this one. Face it, you enjoy having men look at you, wanting you, and they are willing to pay to get that look.

You have bills to pay and this is just a job to get you through hard times and take care of children or pay for college. Nobody even has to know, so you have a stage name, stage clothes and a lifestyle and plan to keep it all separate. You never planned the days that you had to get drunk or drugged just to go inside. The hatred and repulsion of the stench of some was almost unbearable.

I was driving past a topless bar on Highway 57 driving from Arlington Texas into Euless where I worked at the Church, and my heart broke. I had driven by there countless times normally judging "those people," but this day was different. I pulled over and wept for those people working behind closed doors.

I felt compelled often to go and park in the empty parking lot when it would be closed and pray fervently for the women who worked inside. I heard the call. One day something happened, it all changed, it was time; I pulled in, walked right through that front door and said I would like to see the owner.

A young manager walked with me to a back room to see the owner who was seated at a table counting stacks of money. I pretended I did not notice, just like I pretended not noticing women on and off the stage scantily dressed, nor hearing loud pulsating music as I walked past tables of men.

He looked up. I introduced myself as a Chaplain for women and I would like to meet with the dancers and bring them gifts and bless them. I said we would not be there long but wanted to let them know as women we cared. I shared how my own son had taken his life from depression and I did not want to think of any woman not having someone to talk to if they wanted counsel.

It never entered my mind I was not hearing God. It was odd the actual owner was even there. He agreed and let me put up my flier with our contact number in the dressing room. We took gifts once a week and they would lead us directly to the dressing room. I would take one or two ladies with me and instruct them to not stare or appear shocked. I called it the SOB Chaplains Ministry (sexual oriented business).

God was birthing many of this type of outreach in other areas around the world. It was special, scary and edgy, but the passion for souls was greater than the fear of man. Human trafficking is destroying countless innocent children and young girls around the world. It was quite a wakeup call for many.

Amber, a topless dancer from a local club, called and asked me if I would like to attend the grand opening for the newest topless club in Arlington. She thought it would be a great way to meet the new managers and some of the girls who would be working that night. Jesus said to go out into the highways and hedges and to compel people into his kingdom. He went into the homes of tax collectors, prostitutes and sinners and had a meal.

It's about gentlemen's entertainment, flesh, and lust. The old song, "Let Me entertain you," came to my mind. Amber said to everyone around the table, "I want to introduce my friend, Jackie Holland. Jackie is a Chaplain and she is here to meet the managers and some of the girls."

It was always fun to take new people out to do outreaches with me. My friend Brenda Huckins accompanied me to the topless clubs a few times, distributing gifts to dancers. The first time out, I was wondering how she would react going into those clubs. She is a gifted woman so organized in ministry and music and always the perfect lady. I suppose I thought she would be shocked. Brenda flashed that beautiful smile of hers and you would think she was standing in front of school girls. I need to see this type of love. It gives me strength and boldness.

The owner of a totally nude club in far Fort Worth agreed to let us hold Sunday morning church services. We planned on serving free breakfast in their kitchen and offering it to the families of the workers who wanted to attend the Church service. It made so much sense at the time!

The owner of that club agreed and gave us a key to the front door, but, as the devil does, he stirred up threats to the owner. I was later told the disc jockey called a friend from the city. The city council called the owner and would not allow us to hold services there. They cared not that it was geared towards the workers and their families...sad; but I STILL HAVE THE KEY ON MY KEYCHAIN. At least we tried. That is all anyone can do.

Paula Colbath's husband, Mark, brought many gold boxes of Lady Godiva Chocolates to the ministry with a poem and said, "I feel the Lord will minister to the girls with these chocolates."

CHOCOLATES FOR HIS DAUGHTERS

You are always on your Father's heart. He knows you better than you know yourself. While the rest of the world judges you by your appearance, your Father sees the little girl inside you and longs to hold her in his lap. This little girl has been abused by men. The little girl has been forced to grow up and act like an adult. Men have seen your exterior but they never see the little girl. Men lust after the woman and the little girl is not seen. The little girl needs a dad that will hold her in the right way. Your Heavenly Father's love is so strong for that little girl that Jesus came to Earth and died for you. He wants more than anything to express his love for you. He does not express love as men do. He wants to hold the little girl in his lap. He wants to hug you. He wants you to cry on his shoulder. He wants to wipe away every tear. His sole desire for you is that you accept his love and that little girl will live with him forever. No matter how much we sin, Jesus always sees the little child in us. He wants the best for you.

SCRIPTURE PROMISE

Be strong, courageous, and firm; fear not nor be in terror before them, for it is the Lord your God who goes with you: He will not fail you or forsake you.

— DEUTERONOMY 31:6

PRAYER

Dear Heavenly Father, thank you for loving me. Thank you for allowing me to come to you no matter what my past has been. Thank you for making provision at the Cross by sending your only son Jesus to die and pay for the forgiveness of my sins. Thank you, Jesus, for giving me your Holy Spirit to help and guide my life. Forgive me for hurting myself and others. Help me say yes when I need to say yes, and no when I need to say no. Thank you for changing my heart and for forgiving me my sins. Today I confess with my mouth that Jesus Christ is my Lord and my Savior. I am changing into his image daily. I am not ashamed. I am free. I am forgiven. Amen.

20

LOVE, TAKE ME AWAY

Two pictures of the handsome widowed doctor and I together placed side by side on a small shelf under the mirror over the sink in my bathroom… I was so frantic and praying to God for direction and guidance. I didn't love that man. I had begun to wonder if I even liked him. I filled my tub with hot water; crying my eyes out I stepped inside the tub just wanting to wash away all my pain, feeling so trapped.

Ministry… or Marriage?

Marriage in the past had been the answer to all my problems. I wouldn't have to struggle financially if I married. I would have someone to take care of me and be a father to my son Howard who wanted me to marry this man. I would be respected. I would be somebody of value in that town.

God, "Please help me. Show me what to do." I heard a noise and looked up. One of the little pictures fell off the shelf into the sink. I began to wonder, "Lord, what does this mean?" As I was thinking that, the other picture fell off onto my dressing table. I took this as answered prayer and cried out, "Thank you, Jesus!". I don't know what made those pictures fall off the shelf. They had been placed there weeks earlier. But I believe that it was the finger of God. He gave me a sign. I had my answer and peace filled my heart.

A friend called me up and said, "I have a friend coming into town. He is a nice man, a doctor, lots of fun, and yes, he is a single widower. Just dinner. You do not ever have to see him again." I agreed to go.

I was still very fragile and I admit it helped me to get out. He lived out of town and would drive in on weekends and take me out. After just a few dates, he asked me to marry him and gave me an engagement ring. I knew if I married him, it meant I would have to quit the Care Ministry.

My daughter Charlsey was married and doing well. Mike had died, and Howard and I felt so alone. Howard was 15 and needing a man's presence. I knew I could marry him and have a life of ease and "be somebody". This was a very attractive offer to a small town North East Texas girl with four failed marriages, but...I would have to quit my ministry and feeding the hungry in the Mid Cities and pack up and move to Austin!

The answer was no, and after making the decision to not marry I had total peace to keep working at the Care Ministry, having garage sales at my house selling my personal belongings to make ends meet, living alone and looking after my son. I knew very clearly the passion in my heart for the Lord and the feeling I got from helping others needing hope was exactly what made me happy and have meaning in my life.

The superintendent of our school district, a member of our church, said "Jackie, I have the perfect job for you. You will get a full retirement and summers off by working in the Administration office as a secretary." First thought was, wonderful! But, I knew in my heart that I would not take the job. The Lord was not finished with me yet in my ministry work. I called the superintendent that afternoon after church to turn down the job.

I could hear in his voice the thought, "Woman, what is your problem?". You see, this offer was not a bad thing. It just wasn't what the Lord wanted me to do. The safe and easy way isn't necessarily the best way. In life, there will be many distractions, enticements, and choices and not all evil. I believe someone once said that the good choice is the enemy of the best choice. Don't just settle for something seemingly safe.

Ministry is costly. As a single mom and at a time my son was so broken himself after the death of his older brother, he was what you would call a latch key kid. I worked long hours and remember praying… 'Lord, you said you would be a Father to the fatherless, so I have heeded your call and now I trust as I reach out and minister to others children you will watch over my son Howard and be a father to him.'

I have stayed busy in ministry 29 years, and being a single mom and my mother's Care Giver for 10 years and then owning and operating a non-profit Upscale Thrift Store, I have never said life is easy, but exciting, yes. I sense many changes coming in my future. The past 3 years dealing with CLL helps my perspective and I live a thankful life day by day.

Love…people really do not care how much you know until they know how much you care. Real love gives without getting a thank you. Confess over yourself, 'I can do all things through Christ who gives me strength.' Guard your heart. Out of it comes the issues of life, that is what love is all about. You have so much love to give and as you give your love away in his service he will reward you with peace, joy and hope and give you a beautiful future.

SCRIPTURE PROMISE

If I speak in the tongues of men and of angels, but I do not have love, I am a noisy gong or a clanging cymbal. And if I have prophecy, and know all mysteries and all knowledge, and if I have all faith so that I can remove mountains, but do not have love, I am nothing. If I give away everything I own, and if I give over my body in order to boast, but do not have love, I receive no benefit. Love is patient, Love is kind, and it is not envious. Love does not brag, it is not puffed up. It is not rude, it is not self-serving, and it is not easily angered or resentful. It is not glad about injustice, but rejoices in the truth. It bears all things, believes all things, hopes all things, and endures all things. Love never ends.

— 1 CORINTHIANS 13

PRAYER

Dear Heavenly Father, reduce us to love. Let us serve you and others for the same reason, because you told us to love. Teach us to love. Jesus, thank you for loving us so much that you stepped out of Heaven, came into this sinful world, and became a perfect sacrifice for our sins.

Right now, we know you hear our prayer and you defend us from your throne room in Heaven. Because we love you and follow you, we can truly walk in your love. Amen.

21

MIKE'S STORY

I sensed something was wrong. I walked in the house and called out, "Mike, Mike?". I had a strange sinking feeling in the pit of my stomach. I went into my son Howard's room and said, "Where is Mike?". He said, "I think he is in the back yard. His pickup is backed up out there". He said, "I just came in from my friend's house". I will never forget what I saw that night. I looked on the ground and saw my beautiful son lying on his back, arms stretched out to the side. There was his shotgun lying next to him on the driveway. I called out "Mike" and realized he was cold and he was gone. My mind was racing and I said, "Lord, do you want me to call him back from the dead?"... and I heard in my heart, "No, he is with me."

The minutes I spent with my son before I let his brother, and then others know was such a precious time. I hugged him and held him in my arms cradling his body like a child. I told him how much I loved him and how I would not have traded him for anyone else in the world...time stood still for me and the time was my gift from God. Mike was born when I was only 16 and I never dreamed such a thing would happen.

God gave me peace and grace to walk through the valley of the shadow of death and I had no fear of evil. I knew he was with me and he comforted me and helped me to comfort others.

Mike was my prayer partner. Every night he would go outside and sit in his chair under the big oak tree in the front and pray for our family. Mike had a special call on his life for evangelism. Almost every weekend he'd stuff his briefcase full of tracts and spend the day at the mall and hand out small illustrated Christian tracts.

When he wasn't at the mall nothing thrilled Mike more than to take weekend fishing trips with my Daddy. I'd ask, "What do you and Granddad talk about?". "We talk about Jesus and Heaven and what Heaven is like." Daddy had gotten sick and was not able to get out of the house much so that stopped the fishing trips. Looking back, I could tell that Mike seemed sad and lonely and depressed. I prayed over and over that the Lord would send him a good friend.

On November 16, 1989, a cold and damp November day, Mike decided to stay home from work. He had brought home all his tools from work, which was something he had never done before. I figured that he needed to clean them.

"What did you do today?" I asked. "Oh, I went fishing. I didn't catch anything", and he smiled. He looked more rested and relaxed. "I'm so glad you had a good time", I said. "I'm going to music practice tonight at church. Howard's going to a friend's house. If you get hungry why don't you go over to Mother and Daddy's for supper? They'd love to see you." And so, he did.

Sometime after supper and before choir practice was over, Mike took his life. I had no idea that this was to be my last conversation with my son, to look into his blue eyes, hear his sweet voice, feel his presence, smell his hair, and touch his skin.

As a believer, we can have confidence that God loves the hurting, the broken hearted and those held captive. When I say captive, it can be jail or prison, but you can be on the outside feeling like you are in a prison. Pain has no mercy but God does. Depression, they say, is a silent killer.

The reason I want to share Mike's story with you is because you too might be struggling. It could be depression, addiction or fear. Talk with someone who cares about you and will give wise advice. Do not give up, do not lose heart. Trust me, there is always another way, another day, so give God a chance.

Depression can happen to anyone from any walk of life. There is no shame in being depressed. Prayers change things. It is hard for people to believe in miracles but God performs miracles continually in different ways. Medication is not a sin. Get help. People want to help. They just do not know what is going on in your life. You must share with them truthfully.

The Lord gave us the perfect prayer and how to pray, "Thy Kingdom come; thy will be done on earth as it is in Heaven." Praying in agreement in one accord with the Lord's Prayer will release power and might. Just as in Heaven there is no depression or sickness we pray you will be healed of depression or sickness on this earth. No shame. God loves us so much. Tell someone and let them pray with you and believe for your miracle.

SCRIPTURE PROMISE

*Go then and make disciples of all the nations, baptizing them
in the name of the Father and of the Son and of the Holy Spirit,
teaching them to observe everything that I have commanded you,
and behold, I am with you all the days (perpetually, uniformly,
and on every occasion), to the [very] close and consummation
of the age. Amen (so let it be).*

— MATTHEW 28:19-20

PRAYER

Dear Heavenly Father, thank you for life. Thank you for families.
Thank you for children. Dear Lord, even though as parents we
know we have made some bad decisions in times past and may
have set some bad examples for our children, please forgive us.
We love our children and you love our children. Thank you for
loving us just like we are because you love your children and care
for us all the days of our life. We give you thanks and praise.
Draw us near your heart today, and let there be no regrets, no
missed opportunities to make peace, or show love, whenever the
time comes to say our goodbye. Amen.

22

MINISTRY IN PRISON/JAILS

In a moment's time, I had picked up a pistol and pulled the trigger. When I saw the look on his face I knew he was coming to beat me with his bare hands. I shot again and he fell to the floor. At first I thought he was faking, but when I could see he was genuinely injured and it hit me, I frantically called his friend who was a policeman. He called the ambulance and the police came to the house immediately.

He was being carried out to the ambulance and saying she did not mean to hurt me, it was an accident. So, what will happen to me now? My mind was going wild thinking of my children. They took me to the jail, but since he would recover he pressed no charges, and since it was self-defense I was only mugged, fingerprinted and held on a domestic violence charge for just a few hours!

The bullet did not kill my husband and the father of our son, thank God. He would stay a few days in the hospital but I was released to go back home to be with the children. I reminded God that all I had ever wanted was a good marriage and a family. I promised 'I will stay with my husband and never divorce if you will help me.' 15 years later he filed for divorce because he was fathering a child with another woman and our marriage ended.

Divorce and ministry all started around the same time. Howard, my son, had seen the manager of a specialty store in Colleyville Texas throw boxes of excellent produce away. My ministry started in a dumpster on Father's Day. For that I will be eternally grateful.

Broken hearted yet happy, it was sad becoming a divorced woman again but God was using me to be of help to others. Many were hooked on drugs, alcohol and living hard lives out in the world. People needed to know God loves them and has a wonderful plan for their life. God opens a door we either walk through or let fear close the door.

"Jackie…Jackie…" I hear this loud voice calling out my name. I was shopping in Wal-Mart that day. I look up and others had also turned to see what the commotion was about. She yells across the room saying, "Jackie I am going to the jail tonight. Do you want to go with me?"

I did want to do jail visits but was not quite ready, but this time I said OK I will go, thinking it would satisfy Tobra. The drive from Bedford to downtown Fort Worth took about 20 minutes. She was an amazing young woman, a total radical, sort of a hippie dresser and bold as a lioness. I found myself stomping on the brakes but she talked fast and kept my constant attention.

My first visit to the Tarrant County Women's Jail in Fort Worth, Texas was life changing. The regular volunteer said, "Jackie, can you share something about yourself to the ladies?" I opened my mouth and said I shot my husband... They began to yell out to others around them, "she shot her old man". My first captive audience. I shared my story and they understood.

I was so happy but when I walked up the steps to my house I saw my precious little dog, Princess, had gotten run over and she was lying on the steps. In my heart, I felt strongly the devil was mad that I went to the jail.

After being in a car wreck hit from behind I was fearful of a lot of traffic. I would drive on side roads not freeways. After a few evenings of riding with Tobra I insisted I needed to take my turn and drive. I sat on the edge of my seat gripping the wheel in the early evening busy traffic, but after a few times I realized God had taken the fear away. My love for visiting the girls in the jail was greater than my fear of traffic...

That is what the Lord will do for his children. We get in bondage to fear, which is really doubt and unbelief...but we cry to him and he sets us free. So, what the devil intends is to destroy you, but God can turn it all around for your good! I thank the Lord for the friendship of Tobra!

Terry Fancher invited me to minister with him at the Wackenhut Prison in Fort Worth, Texas. I could not believe the freedom in that large gym where over 100 men chose to attend the service. Terry is a great musician singer songwriter, and has such a heart for those incarcerated. I was hooked and went regularly to minister with him...

I invited Tommy Thomas to come to the prison with us. Tommy said, "No way. All these years I have done my best to stay away from those places." He was a new Christian and was on fire for the Lord but he had spent all his life as a professional poker player. When God got hold of Tommy his life turned in a different direction. I said everybody needs to go to the prison at least once; you never have to go back so he agreed but told me... only to observe.

Terry Fancher, Tommy Latham another great singer/ entertainer and minister and I were ministering and God was speaking to Tommy's heart. He said, "Lord, if I have anything to say then show me." He walked up, took the microphone and began to share his story, and the men were moved to tears.

God captured his heart and ever since Tommy has done jail and prison ministry, he even became a published author, he now travels and speaks all over the nation, and has TV programs that go around the world. God sent him a beautiful wife, Latrice, who had been doing jail ministry before she ever met him, they are now a beautiful team.

As one of the Volunteer Chaplains at the Grayson County Jail I minister to hurting women. We all have a "calling" or passion in life. Jail ministry is one of those passions for me. The volunteers share their own amazing stories and pour their hearts out year after year reaching those locked behind bars.

We share with them that if they have prayed the prayer of faith then they are changed within; new person, new identity; given eternal life; forgiven of all sins; the Holy Spirit now lives within them, then we encourage them to pray and spend time with Jesus. Periodically we even have baptisms.

SCRIPTURE PROMISE

Then shall they also answer him, saying, 'Lord, when saw we thee an hungered, or athirst, or a stranger, or naked, or sick, or in prison, and did not minister unto thee?'

Then shall he answer them, saying, 'verily I say unto you, Inasmuch as ye did it not to one of the least of these, ye did it not to me.'

— MATTHEW 25:42

PRAYER

Dear Heavenly Father, thank you so much for the privilege of ministering to hurting people. We are told to go to the highways and byways and tell others about you. Forgive us for being hesitant and bashful about speaking up on your behalf and sharing the simple loving gospel message that sets people free. Give us courage and holy boldness through the power and witness of the Holy Spirit. In Jesus' name we pray. Amen

23

MOTHER HEART OF GOD

I was already planning a trip to Israel. I sensed the Lord saying to me to go as his ambassador and pray for the peace of Jerusalem and for Restoration Church where I was serving. I asked the Lord why and what was his purpose for the love I felt so deeply in my heart for Israel. He directed me to Isaiah 62:6-7: *"I have set watchmen upon thy walls O Jerusalem, which shall never hold their peace day or night. You that make mention of the Lord, keep not silence and give him no rest until he makes Jerusalem a praise in all the earth."* OK. That was my answer; I am a watchman on the wall. This was during the early years of the Care Ministry when I was not receiving a paycheck.

I needed to raise $1850.00 for the Jerusalem trip. Larry Lea Ministries and 300 prayer warriors were going on the trip. I sensed the Lord place in my heart to include a little poem he was giving me along with the details and cost of the trip. I made 10 copies of the letter and poem and passed them out as I felt led.

A lady I didn't know saw me give someone one of the 10 appeal letters. The lady, Sally Knox, asked if she could have one. "Of course,"

I said. The next day she called and said, "I want to go with you." Great, I answered! A few days later Sally called saying, "The Lord told me to pay for your entire trip. He said I can go another time."

Sally confided to me she had argued with him a little because she so wanted to go herself! I gave out the remaining 9 appeal letters and a few other people contributed enough to provide spending money on the trip and any extras!

When Sally gave me her check for the trip she said to me, "I have a scripture for you, Jackie, 'as a mother hen comforts her chicks under her wings, so I will comfort you in Jerusalem.'" Isaiah 66:13. I thought to myself, "How sweet!" But that Scripture didn't mean a whole lot to me at the time. I would leave the day after Christmas 1989 and return a week later.

My firstborn son, Mike, would take his life on November 16th, 1989 and my heart would be broken. I knew the Lord had prepared for me to go to Israel that Christmas by providing for all my needs. Even though after his death I didn't feel like going, I went, and just as the Scripture Sally Knox gave me weeks before, God did comfort me in Jerusalem! I stayed through New Year so it was a new start and a new year coming back home.

A couple of years later Sally and I went back to Israel and we were able to experience it together. She was like a sweet child soaking in the presence of every stop our tour bus made. Sally was a Christian single lady and was an anesthetist at the hospital. Sadly, she became ill with cancer and passed away after a short time.

A lady came to the ministry devastated and heart broken. I closed the door and let her cry on my shoulder until she was able to talk. She began her story telling me her husband had left her for another woman. She said all the years they were married he refused to take her to a movie.

He would not allow her to wear makeup and said she did not need it…but now she discovered he takes this woman he is seeing to the movies and she wears makeup! I was praying while she spoke and asking the Lord to show me how to minister to her and speak into her broken heart.

I shared how the Lord loves her and has a wonderful plan for her life. Her life need not be over. She did her best to please her husband and the Lord would bless her efforts. In the midst of the conversation I asked her if she minded me putting a little makeup on her. She nodded OK looking a bit stunned at my question.

Turning her away from the mirror I took out my makeup bag and proceeded to put foundation, lipstick, blush and eye makeup on her. I got out my comb and began to tease her hair. I sprayed a little spray on it to set the style. All the while I am praying to myself as she is holding back tears.

This was strange ministry. Maybe it had something to do that I loved makeup myself or that I had been a professional hairdresser or maybe because of the abuse in my life and fear of not pleasing my husband, it just happened. When I turned her around to look in the full mirror on the wall at first she looked shocked then she burst out laughing. We laughed and laughed. She looked really pretty.

When she calmed down I told her, 'now you never have to wear makeup again but if you want to you can!' You may never go to a movie but if you want to you can. This woman walked out the door smiling from ear to ear... You are wondering did she ever come back? Yes, once she did stop by and say all was better in her life and she had on makeup.

Another time a lady came to the food ministry for food. She was carrying the child when she came in but she stood him on the floor while she was gathering the selections of food. I noticed he was very bowlegged and his little boots were on the wrong feet. She said it was the only way he could stand upright. I asked if we might pray for healing for her child. She wept and said yes.

My son had to wear braces when he was small to help him stand upright because of his cerebral palsy. I asked the janitor standing nearby to join me in prayer and we cried out for this little boy. The lady was a Tongan woman and it was somewhat hard to understand her language but she was thankful.

She came back again a later time for food and the child's boots were on the right feet and his legs were nearly straight. She said, "Look his legs are straight", and we all began praising the Lord. This mother's heart was rejoicing and I believe the heart of God had compassion on that child that day when we three agreed for his healing and miracle. God loves us so much!

SCRIPTURE PROMISE

Therefore, be imitators of God [copy Him and follow His example] as well-beloved children [imitate their father]

— EPHESIANS 5:1

PRAYER

Dear Heavenly Father, you are God and there is no one like you. I thank you that you are a Father to the fatherless and you care for your children when we suffer and hurt. I thank you for loving us so much you gave your only son to pay the penalty for our sins. We trust in Jesus as Lord and Savior and our very best friend. Thank you for caring about every little detail in our life. Whether we are male or female you love us equally. Just as the mountains surround Jerusalem so shall the Lord surround his people. Amen.

24

SWEETHEART PACKAGE

I wanted to go to the Valentine's dinner, and no, I did not want to take a date or go to serve. However it was for couples only and since it was a regular food distribution evening I worked in the food ministry, a little miffed I might add… thinking you should not be penalized for being single. After all I was one of the Pastors! Little did I know that later that evening a con-man and his wife would walk through those doors and make me one heck of a sweetheart deal that I could not refuse!

I visited a service at The Wisdom Center. The Pastor spoke from the pulpit. "I see Jackie Holland here. She has a beautiful food ministry and we want one so badly. Would you be willing to come and help establish one here?" He had no way of knowing that only a short time before thieves had broken into the offices and we were robbed. They took all our computers and cameras for our TV show. I knew doors were closing so when he asked I nodded yes!

After the service, I spoke with him and told him I would be happy to help but I needed to make a salary so I needed a job.

I still had the ministry in Irving and would need to work both places. He said OK. Since the Lord had allowed me to actually start the food ministry from the ground up I set my own pace, knowing I was responsible.

At the Wisdom Centre, everyone was treated the same. All staff and employees punched a clock, sat in Chapel meetings and did everything by their rules. I had no idea. I was so set and relaxed in my ways, I was in a place where God could humble me and shape me and be in submission to that particular organization. In that one year period, I was stretched, broken and very blessed!

The food ministry was up and running and the Lord allowed me to help set up a monthly luncheon for seniors in nursing homes. We worked with the home coordinators and monthly they brought residents to TWC for a beautiful catered luncheon with gifts for all, music and lots of hugs.

On Valentine's evening a very charismatic man and his lovely wife stopped by the food ministry and asked for a tour. They said they were purchasing an existing church in Lewisville and wanted to have a food ministry and someone said, 'you must go talk to Jackie Holland.'

The next day they showed up at the ministry at the Fellowship International offices. He said, "We believe you would be the person God wants to head up our Outreach Ministries there at Oasis Church." The next day he sent this proposal.

I call this one my sweetheart package. Email sent Feb 27. 2008 from Pastor Nick Mancusso who was purchasing and would be new Pastor of Oasis Church in Lewisville Texas.

'Jackie, it was a pleasure speaking with you today. To reiterate my comments the Church will bring you on staff, pay you an initial salary of $35,000 a year and increase to $50,000 within 12 months. We will move you and your mother to a new home closer to the church and we will pay for that move, as well as for the move of Whosoever Will Outreach Ministries from its current spot to the new location at the Church.

I will provide you an 80/20 medical insurance plan that includes dental and optical. I will place your ministry on the offering envelope, provide a receptacle in the Church foyer for those desiring to sow a seed into your ministry and give you a web page on our site as well. Also free rent for Whosoever Will Ministries and we will pay for the build out in the new space.

We are excited to see what the Lord is about to do in and through your life! We love you!! Let us know if you need anything!! We would love for you to start Easter Sunday.'

Oasis Church on Main Street in Lewisville was huge. The Pastors were Stan and Mandy Dennis, who are very godly precious people. It was an old movie theatre and had so much possibility and the church was already very nice with a coffee bar in the foyer, sofas and a very friendly atmosphere.

I had lived in the Mid Cities area for 32 years, raised my family and it was home. I gave my 2 week notice at TWC and they spoke a prayer and blessing over me when I left that position. My 86 year old mother and I moved there and rented a house down the street from the church.

Every one got insufficient checks and there were many excuses why the money was being delayed for the church purchase, but after a couple of weeks we all figured something was seriously wrong!

I suggested to Pastor Dennis that I knew an attorney in Irving who might help them. I knew he handled a lot of ministry legal issues. It turned out the attorney had prior dealings with this man and everything came to a stop that day. He stated, "I have thick files on Nick Mancuso."

The FBI was contacted immediately and before a week passed Nick Mancuso was in jail. Pastor Nick was not a pastor at all. In fact was a convicted felon who had broken his probation.

After nine months, the church was purchased by Pastor Gregory Dickow's ministry called Life Changers International out of Chicago. They would love for me to stay and volunteer. Sorry. Been there, done that!

God always provides a ram in the thicket. While working at the Wisdom Center my daughter sent a picture by email of a 100 year old home in Sherman. The payments were reasonable and Mother bought her first home in her name at 86.

I had begun another non profit organization called Chaplains for Women International that was birthed during the nine months that I was in Lewisville waiting to see what would happen at Oasis Church.

The ministry did change and we lived on Mother's check and any donations given for the ministry outreach. I stopped any travel so I could care totally for her. I am certain had we remained in the DFW area I would have kept working and never have had the time I had with my mother.

What the devil may have intended for evil God turned around for our good. I had told Mother, "As long as I am alive and well I will take care of you at home and you will never need to go into a nursing home." She liked that. So, God positioned me to be the designated child to care for Mother and for that I am eternally grateful! How could I ever be angry at the Mancuso's for such a gift?

SCRIPTURE PROMISE

Now, Faith is...the substance of things hoped for... the evidence of things unseen.

— HEBREWS 11:1

PRAYER

Dear Heavenly Father, we give you thanks for you do all things well. In this world you said we would have tribulations but you said be of good cheer for you have overcome the world. Lord, we thank you for forgiveness of our sins and we forgive those who have sinned against us. We love and praise you. Let help and healing come to all who have been unfairly used or abused and let faith and mercy be shown. We love you and love others, even those who have hurt us. We wish them well, but most of all for them to know you as Lord and Savior. I pray for salvation for Alias Nick Mancuso and his wife. I forgive and love them. Amen.

25

PROPHETIC DREAMS AND VISIONS

"You will soar on wings like eagles" (Isaiah 40:31), and yes, you will fly! Beautiful flowering plants on running vines growing all around the lattice and arbor covering. Ornate lanterns with flickering clear lights hanging ever so often offering diffused beautiful lighting almost looked like lightening bugs. Seeing it my thoughts I went back in time, remembering as a child in the back yard trying to touch the lightening bugs with their built in twinkling lights. Sometimes we even took old jars and put the lightening bugs inside with a lid with holes in it for air; they just flickered and looked much like those little sparklers Daddy would buy us on the 4th of July. Living in the country there are many advantages like wide open spaces, no smog or big buildings to block your view.

I dreamt that I went to our outdoor Church gathering, in a very pretty setting located in a Brush Arbor type outside pavilion. It was held in the evening. The tables were all lined up for a big banquet filled with all kinds of great food. There were a lot of people there all happy and talking at the same time.

In the dream, sort of standing alone away from the crowd, I saw my Pastor and he looked so disheveled and his face was pale and covered with reddish splotches. He was filled with awe and having an experience with God.

I said, "Brother Doug what is happening?" He answered, "Nothing honey. It's OK." I said, "No please, what is happening to you?" So he stood up, bent over and put both arms straight out to his side and his feet began to come off the ground. He was soaring about 3 or 4 feet off the ground, maybe table top height.

I begged, "Please, Brother Doug, I want to soar also." So, he said, "Now go ahead then and try." So I leaned over, put my arms out, lifted one leg up and then the other followed. I too was soaring.

Soaring out in the open air and high above a river, I looked down and fear gripped me. I remembered I could not swim. I cried out to the Lord and reminded him I cannot swim. 'Did you let me come this far only to let me drown?' The Lord knew my anxious thoughts and he took me over to the dry ground, I landed beautifully on my feet…it was glorious.

A few curious ones said, "Here, let me try", but they were just floundering around flapping their arms and legs but not really getting anywhere. About that time Larie, the Pastor's wife, had arrived late and she walked in and said, "Oh, what is happening? I want to soar also", but I woke up.

Early on in the ministry I dreamt of being in the back seat of a vehicle and my child was being born; I was thinking, 'oh no, I do not know who the Father is', but the baby came. I actually cut the cord myself. Oddly in the dream the little girl stood wobbly legged to her feet like maybe a 1 or 2 year old year old and she was adorable.

Pretty blonde hair, little curls and suddenly people were around saying, "Awe, so beautiful", and then she took steps and was crippled and the people said, "Oh no". They were visibly disappointed but the Lord showed me, 'Look, she can walk', so the people said, "Aye, that is good."

I noticed she had an eye in the center of her forehead and the people saw it too and they said, "oh no", but I pulled her bangs down and said, "Look it is covered". So the people said, "Awe, that is good". I think it represented the ministry and I felt so imperfect, looking crippled and wobbly but I had been given discernment from the Lord, but needed to not show off. I have not forgotten that feeling. Oh yes, the most important part, the Father of the little girl was the Father of us all!

I walked into a room with all young mothers. They all had babies and their little faces were covered. I rushed over and said, "Oh, I want to see", and pulled back the blankets one after the other...they were all baby lionesses. I was shocked I tell you, shocked. But then I said, "They look just like their father. After all he is the Lion of the tribe of Judah."

Interesting that lionesses do not have all that huge mane of hair but these were baby girls and they looked like their Father's full mane! Maybe a year after my dream I was so excited to purchase and read Lisa Bevere's book about lionesses arising.

God can and does use various ways to speak to us, dreams and visions, answered prayers, and in that still small voice like a whisper he says, "I love you." Show us your glory, O Lord, the glory of the Lord. Is not this what you have been asking the Lord for? Is that not the cry of your heart?

Well, I believe he is saying, "Open your eyes... Look up. Your redemption is drawing near ... He is near ... even at the door. Behold the fields.... are they not white unto harvest? Has he not begun a great shaking on this earth? But you say, it must be this way or that way, and yet he says, I am the way. I will do my work however I choose to do it; I will turn the hearts of the fathers to the children. I will cause such a stirring in hearts, showing my wondrous works. People from every race and from culture and every economic position will see. Eyes of understanding, ears that want to hear are opening, scales will fall off eyes.

Because I am doing a work and I am changing lives and hearts I and I alone deserve praise, reserve your praise only for me", says the Lord. "You know and must always remember I Am the Lord and I change not.

Just glorify me in everything you do if you want to make me happy....

As you open your mouth let praise for me fill the air ... Yes, I hear your praise.

I love your praise, I will do the work, and I will call my chosen ones out."

SCRIPTURE PROMISE

But those who wait for the Lord [who expect, look for, and hope in Him] shall change and renew their strength and power: they shall lift their wings and mount up [close to God] as eagles [mount up to the sun]: they shall run and not be weary; they shall walk and not faint or become tired.

— ISAIAH40:31

PRAYER

Dear Heavenly Father, I thank you for giving us your best; you are the giver of life, hope and salvation. You have made so many of our dreams come true. You know what our needs are. Thank you for watching over us and keeping us in the palm of your loving hands.

Fill us with your Holy Spirit and your power. Help us to stay focused on you and to love unconditionally without seeking notice or rewards but love because you first loved us. Thank you, Jesus. Show us your Glory! Let your goodness pass before us, right before our eyes. We love and adore you. In Jesus' name we pray. Amen.

26

TURN A MESS INTO A MESSAGE

I stood with my heavily starched white uniform with my cute little nurse's cap pinned on perfectly coifed hair all ready for the day, looking the part in my early 20's, trying to get through the classes and become a Licensed Vocational Nurse. Excited about my turn to do ER work at the hospital, one morning they brought a man in from a car accident who was actually bleeding to death. The doctor was working furiously on this man as he was losing his life because of so much blood loss. As the doctor was tying off veins in his leg, I stood there watching the blood drip out of that man's body. Drip, drip. The stench of alcohol mixed with blood was too much for me. I had always had a weak stomach. I felt lightheaded. It got so bad I told the doctor, "I think I am going to faint." He yelled back, "Keep working, this is no time to faint." When he saw I was serious he told me to sit down and put my head between my knees, and that's all I remember. When I came to I heard the doctor yelling, "Get her out of here. Get me another nurse." That did it for my nursing career!

I felt so foolish that I could not bring myself to go back. I only needed one month to graduate. In nursing training, you had the classes and then the practical work at the hospitals and nursing homes. Every week we had different assignments and patients that we assisted the nurses with so as to learn the appropriate care of the patients.

I enjoyed things like taking the food trays to people and making their beds, but needles and dirty soiled diapers were a different matter. I shall never forget the nurse saying, "Go remove Mr. So and So's catheter", a very fragile elderly man; but what she did not know and what I failed to ask was, how do you do that?

My mother loved nursing and had no problem with a weak stomach. Following her advice, I had pursued my career in nursing. I was a divorced woman with two small children, so young and so shy and fearful, trying to find my place in life.

You must decide your own future, not your mother's or others' who want to help. Yes, get counsel and seek wisdom from God but ask God to show you his plans and purpose, and do those things.

I attended Cosmetology School in Paris, no, not Paris France but Paris Texas. Again this took me West, unlike East with the ammunition plant where I had worked and been in that hand grenade explosion when my ear drum busted from the blast, nor the nursing training in the Texarkana area. This was West, the other direction.

One bad relationship after another, taking different classes and jobs, yet I still felt like a loser. God knows, I wanted to change but felt powerless. The need to be loved and accepted was greater than my weakness to hurt. You may say, 'I am powerless to change, and besides this life is all I know. If I change I lose my friends and my life would be so boring. I do not want to get old and have not lived!'

I understand you are hurting and abused right now. There is healing going into your spirit. I speak new life into you. I speak deliverance to you in the name of Jesus Christ. I pray restoration into you. In the mighty name of Jesus, in the undefeatable, all powerful, everlasting name of Jesus, I proclaim victory for you.

Turn your mess into your message, your test into a testimony. You know how others feel and what they are experiencing. That very well could make all your hardships worth going through when you know God has empowered you to speak into another's life, one hurting broken and in despair. You can show the love of God is powerful enough to not just change a heart but change a life and destiny.

No education or credentials can change a life; but by using your own life experiences you become the counselor that can offer change. In fact forget the degree right now, just please God and love people, makes amends where you can, let go of past hurt and unforgiveness. There is new life ahead for you. God is for you, totally and completely. Believe me on this. I know from experience! Your test will become a powerful testimony.

Repenting means that, as you are confessing your sins, you are admitting that they are wrong and that you must turn from them. Your attitude becomes, "I must make some strong corrections in my life. *I have been wrong.*" You may have tried this before on your own, and couldn't do it. The difference this time is to ask Jesus to be with you. Only he and the Holy Spirit can give you the power to make it work. Ask him for deliverance and help.

One by one you will be able to give those sins, addictions and bad habits up. Not by your power but by asking God to intervene and help. Trust me again here. He will turn your mess into a message and give you the power to say yes when you need to say yes, and say no when you need to say no. Just trust him today. Trust him and take that leap of faith and move into your amazing future!

SCRIPTURE PROMISE

Seek the Lord while he may be found, call on him while he is near.

— ISAIAH 55:6

PRAYER

Dear Heavenly Father, so many times I tried on my own and failed, yet you never walked away and said, "I do not love you." When I finally realized you really truly do love me, I gave you my life, because you opened my spiritual heart to believe. Thank you so much for your love. I ask for my sister or brother praying this prayer, Holy Spirit, fall upon them now and let them too know the height, the depth, the width of your love that can reach further than they could ever imagine. Right now, dear Lord, bring joy and hope and turn their messes into their message and their tests into their testimony and use them greatly for your name's sake. In Jesus' name we pray. Amen.

27

TRASH TO TREASURE

I opened the classified section of the Fort Worth Texas Star Telegram as I did every day and looked to see what was being sold or bartered. A lady had a massive eight carat dinner ring for sale. The way she described it made my mouth water. I had hoped to do some trading but she actually just wanted the money…however, I asked her why on earth would you sell a ring like that? She said, "Honey, when I was your age I loved to get all dressed up and go dancing, wear beautiful clothes and my flashy diamond jewelry."

She added, "Honey, when you get to my age there is really just one thing in life that makes you excited." She had my undivided attention and I asked, "Really? What is that?" Her response, "A really good BM!" Oh dear, that was shocking. I had not expected such a ridiculous answer. We did not make a trade but I tell you I have laughed about that many times and to be honest, at this stage in life, I understand her comment totally.

We have seen the bumper stickers 'I brake for garage sales.' Ok, I am guilty. I might see what looks like a perfectly good piece of furniture sitting on the curb. This antique table is broken, but just look at the legs. I rush back to my truck, grab a couple of tools and begin to remove antique chair legs or handles and knobs.

People are passing by looking intently my way. Ha, ha, I beat you to them; I bet they wish they had found this first! Decisions, decisions...sometimes I just glance at stuff and think, "No, I am going to leave that for someone else that may really need it." How noble of me! The joy of the treasure is in the initial discovery.

Hidden treasures are just waiting to be discovered by you. I have been in a garage sale actually holding an item in my hand only to hear someone call out across the room, "That is mine. I saw it first." You don't kid around with serious shoppers when they are on a quest; stay out of their way or suffer the consequences. The experienced thrift shopper knows all the tricks and strategies of haggling, buying or even reselling their items.

Take caution with personal care items...I went to a garage sale and purchased what I thought was a very expensive serum for the hair. It was at a fraction of the cost and I could hardly wait to saturate my hair. I put on a heavy amount of the hair serum and within minutes it had glued my hair together in a ball! Someone must have added some type of glue for pure meanness. It took a long while and a lot of effort to dissolve that product without breaking off every hair on my head.

Growing up, Daddy was the water commissioner and it was located right next to the city dump. He would bring in small pieces of furniture or interesting collectibles. One day I walked there with him and sure enough someone had thrown out a load of trash. Within that trash was some real treasures. I was hooked.

Mother was not impressed at all. She was embarrassed, hoping the neighbors had not seen us. I recall her saying, "What are you doing with all that junk?" Mother had grown up during hard times and had sacrificed a lot for us kids to have the best. Even if they were homemade cotton sack dresses they were the latest patterns, so for her to think people in that small town might see us digging in their trash she was horrified.

I think Daddy's laid back attitude and gratitude for those experiences set me up to enjoy the discovery of making treasure from trash...I wish he were alive to see how excited people get over old doors and industrial plows and tools, old windows and headboards.

TV programs are drawing huge audiences of people learning to create unique and useful items out of what looked like typical junk, then by adding or taking something off they make it into a whole new purpose. You can spend hours watching people turn trash into little treasures, stories like the person who bought an old dirty picture and it turned out to be a masterpiece.

Shows like *Strange Inheritance* or *Pawn Stars* and even *Flipping Houses* are similar, because everything is about profit and smart shopping. Investors take old houses, restore them and sell them at a large profit.

YouTube is a treasury of "how to do anything" and offers videos on how to do projects from A to Z. If you have questions the internet will give you answers, but beware of the clutter and trash that is mingled inside. Be wise but search. Your answers are there.

Tips for shopping are to just be wise and alert...*Craigslist* and other online groups, sales and auctions...Search the areas. Yes, you can haggle with the price, but respond to the seller in a normal courteous way. To get a rapid response say something like, "I am very interested in the item and have cash. Can you call me?" That way you have their number. Generally people like wheeling and dealing, so just tack on a little extra on your start price when selling.

God is the Creator of everything. He knows first hand how to take a piece of clay and create a man, then take a rib from the man and create a woman...and the rest is history. It is in our DNA to create and be resourceful with our time, talents and money. Your gifts and talents will indeed make a place for you and set you before kings and priests. Creating stuff for you, or for sale, is fulfilling, fun and rewarding.

Oh, by the way, when you are tired of your old junk let me know. It may be just what I have been looking for...happy hunting!

SCRIPTURE PROMISE

How precious is your steadfast love, O God! The children of men take refuge and put their trust under the shadow of your wings.

— PSALM 36:7

PRAYER

Dear Heavenly Father, thank you for loving us so much. You loved us so much you sent your son Jesus Christ to give his life to pay for our sins. Thank you for salvation, deliverance, healing, mercy and grace. Thank you for not throwing away the clay. You are the potter so mold us, shape us into a more beautiful useful person than we could ever have imagined. We love you so much, Amen.

28

LOVE ME TO THE MOON AND BACK

Now that he is gone, I want a white house, and a picket fence. I want those awful blue side windows and front doors changed to something more open, light and happy. I remember standing at the corner of my driveway surveying our home and thinking, 'this is not a very pretty house. It's a nice house but it's not a pretty house. The brick is orange and it has black shutters.'

In fact the trim on the house was black. There were wrought iron bars on all the windows and the front porch light was cobalt blue.

My husband got the house through a trade purchase with Larry Cole, the former Dallas Cowboy who had become a builder in that area. Guess what I thought…I am going to paint this house white. My husband is gone. He cannot tell me what to do and I do not have to get his permission.

I want a white picket fence and flowers running on my fence. I want lots and lots of flowers. I will have a wishing well in my yard and plant all kinds of roses. For the first time, it occurred to me that I was my own responsibility. That meant I had to live with my own decisions and I was now the bread winner at that house. Someone (probably a guy) mentioned it might bring the property value down to paint the brick, 'Who cares?' I thought!

Somewhere in between handing out food and trying to rebuild my life as a once again single mother, I discovered that repairing and restoring my now broken home became very important. I had always loved taking care of the inside. In fact, I remember making the decision to paint the dark wood paneling a soft pink tone and covered the walls with huge mirrors while my husband was out of town. It went from dark Mediterranean style to modern overnight.

When I decided to write this chapter dealing with the changes in one's life after divorce, I hardly knew where to start. Even though I had four failed marriages I can hardly remember them, but my daughter reminded me of the changes that took place in my life after my fourth marriage fell apart.

Fifteen years invested (in what I thought were the best years of my life) but not wasted, I was learning to lean on the Lord and the children and I had always prayed for their dad and step dad every day. They believed in the power of prayer. We prayed over broken toilets and lawn mowers that would not start. My children became prayer warriors.

Divorce is a type of death... of dreams and what could have been. Divorce is like a death – but with the corpses still walking around. Approximately one out of two marriages ends in divorce. These broken marriages leave a trail of broken dreams.

Divorce is the death of intimacy and trust between a man and a woman. It is the ripping apart of a huge emotional investment as well as God's will for a man and a woman. Each of us is a spiritual vessel. Some of our vessels carry pure gold, others silver or bronze, others carry garbage. Still others are empty. When our vessels become crowded with debris from divorce, we tend to see every situation through all this debris. It becomes like a filthy screen. We can hardly see through it.

If you are single (or suddenly single), consider that God has separated you to be single at this stage of your life for a new work and even ministry. God has put something in you to attract, to share. Single people have opportunities to draw close to God in ways that married people never can. Often, they have the luxury of time.

God's will is doing what the Bible says. That is all. As you do that, opportunities will present themselves. If you want to go deeper into his will, do that in a big way. Follow the advice of Oswald Chambers. "Have faith and do the next thing." Divorce recovery is not about who was to blame or who failed.

To forgive is not to develop amnesia. It is to reach a place where the misery is pulled out of your memory. Here is God's way of de-clawing the past: pray for the person who hurt you. Pray for their salvation. This is what God's forgiveness is all about, prayer for goodness in your own soul.

When we are young, we have a clear conscience. The older we get the duller our conscience becomes. Our actions do have consequences. You are too important to throw your life away in sin addictions or the bottle trying to drown away your troubles. It only creates more hurt in life.

You can survive the effects of divorce and recovery because of the Cross, the dying to self, re-birth, and resurrection back to a holy life with Christ. It is a wonderful experience which takes us back to who we were intended to be by God.

Come back to God's ways for a new beginning, a fresh start. The old passed away and all things start over. Leave that baggage behind, you will not need it as a crutch or a burden, it is a new day. God loves you so much; you are free to be you!

SCRIPTURE PROMISE

For all who are led by the Spirit of God are sons of God. For [the Spirit which] you have now received [is] not a spirit of slavery to put you once more in bondage to fear, but you have received the Spirit of adoption [the Spirit producing son-ship] in [the bliss of] which we cry Abba (Father)! Father!

— ROMANS 8:14-15

PRAYER

Dear Heavenly Father, I thank you for new opportunities and chances to live my life. I thank you that my past will not dictate my future. I thank you that you love me and want me to excel in my life and in my calling and profession. Whether I am single or married does not have any effect on your love for me. Every good and perfect gift is from above and we say thanks once again. Show us your perfect way. I am not a divorced woman or man. I am a child of God highly favored and loved. My future is hopeful because you said, 'I give you hope and a future.' In Jesus' name we pray. Amen.

29

THE GREAT COMMISSION

I had four failed marriages. I was no poster child for women in ministry. Then I think about the despised Samaritan woman at the well who had the encounter with Jesus and became an evangelist in one day! We do not have to strive for a place; he will make a place when you use the gifts he already placed inside you.

Connecting my ministry dots… the Lord connected me on my ministry journey using Evangelist James Robison. He had shared on TV that he was part of a new church plant meeting at the Bell High School in Bedford Texas. We lived just down the street from the school. I loved the service immediately that very first day. At the end of the service someone was calling out things like, 'I have an extra washer, does anyone need it?' Someone saying, 'Yes', and others calling out lots of really nice items, I think even a vehicle.

They said, "If you need money when the plate is passed take out what you need." That was unheard of…surely this was Revival and in a high school with several ex- Baptist Pastors and Deacons at that. They had been touched mightily by the power of God and filled with the Holy Spirit and he had turned their lives around! It was contagious. I tell you the truth! Like a fire it spread and we all jumped in to catch the glory of God's Presence being given to us by the Lord.

In every story there is a beginning...In the summer of the 1980's Dr. Douglas C. White, a man of God for over two decades, was called to begin a small fellowship among twenty people, leading them in Bible study, prayer, and worship which was named Mid-Cities Baptist Fellowship. In a short time the group merged with Lake Country and they started meetings held at Bell High School in Bedford Texas.

After visiting the church a few times the Lord was powerfully dealing with my heart on reaching the needy and helping hurting broken people. In 1985 I made an appointment to see Pastor Doug White. I shall never forget sharing my heart, weeping and sincerely seeking his direction. He was so calm and fatherly. I remember thinking that at the time, 'I know he can be trusted.'

When Pastor Doug had laid hands on me he did not know anything about me. He just knew that I was very sincere. I asked him to pray for me to know what to do and how to do it and he did. He prayed a beautiful prayer that the Lord would use me in his work and he would raise up people to help me do the work and fulfill the calling on my life.

When my grandson Isaiah was born his Daddy, who did not attend that church, was determined to have James Robison anoint his son Isaiah with oil and dedicate him to the Lord. He was happy to bless him. Isaiah is married with two children and they lead a home group and are very active in their church.

During those times we were introduced to Robert Morris, a young minister with a love for the Lord. Only God knew that one day he would pastor one of the largest Megachurches in the DFW area and others at many locations. Even odder, I am a member of his church though not active, living in another city.

Two years later, on Father's Day 1987, the food ministry was birthed. Pastor Doug White was not only my Pastor but he was now my boss. They found a near vacant shopping center in Euless, Texas and selected the site of an abandoned hardware store, renovated it, and in 1985 named it Restoration Church.

I was on staff there 15 years as Care Ministry Pastor. The main sanctuary was where the Euless Bowling Alley was located and for years I had been on a weekly bowling league right there. Then to become one of the Staff Pastors in that very place, that could only be God!

A friend said, "Jackie, I have a neighbor whose son was in a accident and he is paralyzed from the neck down. She is a Christian and is praying God will heal him. Can we go by her home and you pray for him? I know he can be healed." "Yes indeed", I said, so we went inside. The mother happily allowed us to see her son and we talked just a minute then my friend asked, "Can Jackie pray for your son? She is in ministry."

The mother looked at me again more intently, then asked, "Are you a licensed minister?" I said, "Not yet, but I love Jesus and have seen him heal many and I do full time ministry and believe in healing." She pulled back and answered, "No, I would rather you not pray. I only want licensed ministers to pray for my son."

What if that could have been a divine appointment for healing for her son but was not allowed simply because of credentials? I did receive my credentials and realized they are not for the person ministering but for the trust and confidence for those receiving!

To preach means to proclaim the good news. Jesus is the message; we are the messengers. The power in our message is not our own but there is power in the blood of Jesus. Jesus said, "I will not leave you comfortless. I will send my Holy Spirit who will lead you and guide you into all truth."

Peter had been a fisherman, but he spent three years with Jesus as a follower, and when Jesus was gone Peter opened his mouth and the Holy Spirit gave him the words to share where 3,000 souls were saved that day, changed by the gospel message. Woman or man…preach the power of Jesus. I remember back in the early 80's President Reagan challenged everyone to read their Bible every day.

We all have a story and God will use your story to build up and encourage others in your life and ministry. Kathryn Kuhlman said God is not looking for golden vessels or silver vessels, he is looking for yielded vessels! The healing ministry comes in many forms. The human touch is powerful.

By faith, we can speak for the Lord; admonish, exhort, edify and comfort others with godliness and good works. The power is the anointing of the Holy Spirit as promised by Jesus after the resurrection. It is the power to serve God. Experience God's presence and spend time with the Lord in prayer and the Word.

SCRIPTURE PROMISE

"The Spirit of the Lord is upon me; because the Lord hath anointed me to preach good news to the meek, to preach the acceptable year of the Lord, to comfort those who mourn, to give them beauty for ashes, the oil of joy for mourning, the garment of praise for the spirit of heaviness".

— ISAIAH 61:1-3

PRAYER

Heavenly Father, I come to you in the name of Jesus. I am here and now repent for my sins, and believe in Jesus Christ, the Son of God. I believe that Christ died for me, as my substitute, and rose from the dead according to the Scriptures. Thank you, God, for sending your Son, and paying my debt in full. Whosoever shall call on the name of the Lord shall be saved. I declare by faith that Jesus Christ now lives in me. I am a new creation in Christ, born of God with the life of Jesus in me. According to Your Word, I am now forgiven, I am now saved. Amen.

30

UPSCALE THRIFT AND DESIGNS

We came down to board up the windows. Glass was everywhere. Howard's original Ronald McDonald had been a window display, now standing in the open window waving at passers by; poor thing, part of his skin shaved off his fiberglass body, from the broken glass. Some guy had knocked all our front windows out. Having a small business has many struggles but people never know because they are looking for great deals and hidden treasure and we aim to please!

A sweet customer came in the thrift store and noticed the huge stained glass window my son had bought as she was leaving the store. I told her that my son had bought it for me but it was so large it covered our front store walls. She said, "I have a thought. I wonder if my son would have any interest. He is building a huge new home." She called him on the spot and explained about the stained glass. He told her he was sitting with the architect who had just told him the ceiling was extremely high. He really needed a window or something that would reflect the light and height of the ceiling. She sent pictures and my son sent measurements and it was a great sale.

God knew it needed to be in a safe place. The huge stained glass window from the old church was sold to Hunter Smith, singer songwriter, motivational speaker and former NFL football player.

Perfect. That made us happy that he and his wife loved it and now proudly display it in their beautiful new home. He said they constructed lights inside it and it is the first thing people see when they enter the front door; they look up and see the cross.

They brought a huge covered trailer and loaded up the window. We had a lovely visit. They are a great couple who love the Lord and it was such a blessing for the cross to go to the place God intended. We were simply the 'go to' place to make that happen. Before they drove off I gave her a copy of my book *Exposed Heart*.

She called me a couple of days after getting home and said it was such an excellent book. She read it out loud to her husband as they traveled home to Indiana. She ordered 20 books so she could give them as gifts to her friends. Funny, but people like this family is what makes being in a small business worthwhile. I love their stories.

I called him and asked if I could share this story, and of course he said absolutely. He said they love the window and his wife is a big Jackie fan! How fun, a happy satisfied customer.

I like hearing people get excited and say I can't believe I got rid of this or that thing. Now they want it again. Shoppers get excited to recreate their childhood memories that they had held so dear.

I was Mother's care giver and it was hard at first to let her go. I was grieving and really didn't feel like making decisions on my future just yet. I knew I needed to decide fairly quickly to move back to the DFW area or start looking for a job.

My daughter said, "I can give you a year if you want to open a thrift store to benefit the ministry." My son dropped everything to help, doing all the hauling, loading, painting. It was a beautiful thing Upscale Thrift Store in Sherman, Texas. My first and only experience, setting up a store.

My son, my daughter and my son-in-law were all painting walls, pulling out old carpets, opening doors and walls and shelving, laying carpet and hanging chandeliers. We were working together and growing closer together every day. I told my daughter I did not know how to use a cash register. She laughed and said, "Just think of it as a garage sale!" I could do that.

I respect that my children and family have stood behind me as I was trying to obey the Lord and do it all with excellence. They agreed we felt we should give our best as unto the Lord.

My brother Don and two sisters Barbara and Marita pitched in and gave me the small inheritance money Mother left us to put it in the store to buy furniture, décor and accessories. My daughter, son and I worked to build a beautiful thrift store packed for treasure hunters.

After one year my daughter Charlsey and her husband Jeff sold their property in Sherman and moved to Tennessee, so the store became mine and my son Howard's responsibility.

Count the cost...At a time when most people kick back and

retire I found myself in marketplace ministry. Trust me, it is different than being on staff at a church...stretch! Because we handpick items for the store, I make so many trips to Goodwill. If I skip a few days, they come check on me!

Upscale or Junky Atmosphere... some people like lots of junk to dig through, others want it more tidy. I particularly love less chaos, maybe because of having so much in my life. Buy, sell and trade... try to please the customer... be kind...learn the art of the deal; haggle.

Time for action. It's a movement...18-20 % of Americans shop in thrift stores. Pinterest, Etsy, Blogs, Craigslist, countless porch and garage and estate sales; it is the going thing. Google agrees, "Vintage is hot right now." It became obvious to me that people were so excited to recreate their childhood memories that they had held so dear.

If I had been in the Dallas Fort Worth area it would have been simple to just get the word out and receive donations, but I found here in this smaller town if you do not have a church behind you then you are truly on your own.

Bejeweled Guitars...I had bought a guitar that was not that valuable from a guy needing money. I looked over at the jar full of off white small screws and it seemed right to get out my hot glue gun and beautify that old guitar. Oddly enough the screws looked like pearls. I have made at least 100 guitars all different and unique, many on display. People always make comments like, say, 'Miranda Lambert or the Road Show needs to come to your place.'

Repurposing, painting, sanding, plugging holes, tightening screws, it's all part of the assignment of having a successful furniture thrift store. I know we have gone through hundreds of cans of paint and dozens of paint brushes.

At your business, do not be afraid to share your faith, for fear that you will lose clients or box yourself into only one audience. It is always right to respect and honor people and their beliefs. Opportunities arise, and you will have the chance to speak life and hope to another person.

For the last three years, after being diagnosed with Chronic Lymphocytic Leukemia stage four, I have now talked with countless people who have or have had cancer or had a loved one or friend with cancer so we have had some serious discussions on this matter.

We have cried, prayed and laughed together. The regular customers seem to love my good progress and they watch to see my outcome. Of course, I always tell them what the Lord said… "You shall live and not die but declare the works of the Lord!"

Enjoy your shopping experience. You can dress with the best, save money, get great junk and good quality clean designer bargain shopper items. It will always be fun because you are looking for that surprise inside… it's a collector's dream scenario.

I am glad the thrift stores have caught on and I believe we helped to inspire others, but truthfully since we buy outright we worked ourself almost out of business. I must remind myself, "In ministry that is what you are supposed to do!" Encourage, edify comfort and exhort others to godliness and good works! Ministry in the Marketplace.

SCRIPTURE PROMISE

The LORD shall open unto thee his good treasure, the heaven to give the rain unto thy land in his season, and to bless all the work of thine hand: and thou shalt lend unto many nations, and thou shalt not borrow."

— DEUTERONOMY 28:12

PRAYER

Dear Heavenly Father, thank you for your wonderful provision and gifts, providing for every area of our life. We thank you for your love and for your watching care over us and all that concerns us. Thank you for wanting us to prosper and be in health even as our soul prospers. You are our provision. Thank you for great surprises along life's way. You said that in all our ways if we ask you, then you will guide our steps. We love you, Jesus, Amen.

31

MIGHTY MAN OF VALOR

Congratulations, you are pregnant...yes, surprise was a understatement from my doctor's visit because I was taking birth control pills regularly. It hit me like a slap in the face, but in a good way. My whole world turned around in a day. I was beside myself with joy. After three failed marriages I so wanted this one to work. When I found this out for the first time in years I had hope and it felt like the Lord was blessing me and letting me make up for my bad mistakes in life. This child was my second chance in life.

Charlsey was 10 and Mike was 12 and my two stepchildren living with us were Harold the third 5 and Priscilla 3 $^1/_2$ years, all anxiously waiting for our own little baby boy. The children and I loved shopping for baby clothes, bassinet and blankets. I remember us taking out the baby powder, baby magic and oils just to smell them and sometimes we would hold those tiny diapers up and say, 'Can you imagine little legs sticking through here?'

I knew God had his hand on this boy named Howard Holland; he was so loved by us all. It seems to me some people are just bigger targets for the devil to attack, and Howard was one of them. He has his own story and I will not tell it but will say that the devil has tried to take him out many times in life.

When he was fifteen a lady pulled in front of him while on his motorcycle and broke his leg. He has had a slightly longer leg because it just stopped growing. During that time he got bleeding ulcers in his stomach and had to stay in the hospital trying to heal from that, not just the broken leg. ...a few years later he began suffering with Crone's and has ulcers that flare up fairly often.

As a single mom life had many ups and downs trying to be both mother and father. I admit I did not do the best job. I was sold out to helping hurting people that I spent 8-10 hours a day 6 days a week at the ministry. I remember praying, "Lord, you know I have answered the call to minister to the hurting and help provide food for needy families, so while I am taking care of others children you said you would be a Father to the fatherless, so I am counting on that from you for my young son Howard."

The food ministry was actually started by Howard...he did not realize it at the time nor did I, but God knew exactly what he was doing. Once I asked God how he sees Howard, and he said, "I see a mighty man of valor!" One year he and his friends were out and he took something that was highly allergic and almost died. In fact the doctor had him on life support and said, "Come if you want to see your son while he is still alive"... but God had his hand on him.

Another time, he was out of town working and was robbed and beaten almost to death. He had concussion and had been left for dead when found and hospitalized. He has expressed he has problems remembering at times and I feel certain it was from that horrible beating.

Some of you know the feeling there will be one in a family that seems to get hit harder than others. I do not know why, I think that happened to me also. Perhaps it was because we were the baby, the youngest of the children. So many times, let's face it, we spoil the youngest. What the first ones got corrected and disciplined for, the last gets away with scot free!

Howard and I have had a lot of close hard experiences. He and I were the first to find Mike dead from probable suicide. Many years later he lived in another state and came back to visit Grandma, and she died the day he visited as he and I held her hand.

My daughter Charlsey and her husband Jeff moved to Tennessee. Her son Isaiah Bock is married to Brittany Vines Bock and they have two beautiful children (my great grandchildren) Scarlett and Bearon, both adorable.

Howard stayed in the area and helped me with keeping a thrift store going and stepping up and saying he would take care of me when I am sick with the cancer diagnosis. That is why I want you to know Howard and keep him in your prayers.

Howard has three beautiful daughters, Cierra, Alexis and Dallas. I pray for them to be mighty women of God. I have never been able to spend much time with them but I love them very much and am so proud of their accomplishments. They are all uniquely beautiful and I pray they are happy and blessed.

I made so many messes in my younger years but God forgives and forgets. We are all broken in one way or another. Troubles and trials come to all. Do we get better or bitter? It seems to me, as Christians, God will take all those things that the devil tried to destroy you with and turn them around for your good.

The Bible says those who are forgiven much love much. Perhaps it brings out the compassion because you may know how it feels to be broken, rejected and thrown aside; but the potter picks up that broken clay and reshapes it and makes it more durable and beautiful than ever.

God loves your family and cares about what you are struggling with today. It could be addictions or strongholds in certain areas. There is nothing too hard for the Lord.

God makes beautiful things out of dirt. Just look around at his creation. We, my friend, are a work in progress. God is not through using you. Sometimes we can be really hard on ourselves and if not dealt with have secret shame, thinking we do not match up to our own expectations, much less others'. That is what happens with sin. There is pleasure in sin for a season but always with consequences.

God does not call the qualified, he qualifies the called. Scars are like badges. Do not be ashamed. When the Lord forgives he forgets, so quit beating yourself up. He says we are his beloved, cherished, a joint heir with Jesus Christ. God uses ordinary people in extraordinary ways.

The Master's touch on the potter's wheel. Many times, the potter will take old clay that was once cracked, shattered, or broken, ugly and no longer of value and grind it into dust then moisten it with water before he puts it on his wheel. He then shapes it into a vessel he is pleased with. All of the old ugly cracked and broken pieces disappear as it is molded and shaped into something beautiful. It is still very fragile and the clay still soft and pliable, the color dull and drab.

So, the potter places the vessel into the fiery kiln, carefully keeping his eye on it as he processes it in the burning heat. When he senses sufficient time in the hot oven he removes it, then displays its beauty and places it on a shelf for others to see and appreciate.

I think that is what he does in our life. He allows the fires of affliction to come and burn out and bring to the surface all of the ugly sinful things in our life so we will repent of those sins and failures.

He determines what we need and knows when we are willing to decrease and allow him to increase in our life. The potter will take out the vessel from the furnace. Then the heat will have radically transformed a broken, even shattered, clay vessel into a vessel of strength, glory, multicolored beauty and honor.

Two years ago Howard negotiated the sale of our Thrift store and with the sale we got free rent for a year. That was such a blessing because that was at the time I was really having the active cancer symptoms going on, so it took a lot of pressure off.

When our store windows were all knocked out, Howard took charge and handled all the cleanup and necessary hauling. He and I believed the man should not be prosecuted; he was cold and wanted the police to pick him up and take him to jail. The poor man was drunk but he was tired.

Howard has literally taken car loads of clothes from his own closet and given them away, toys for needy children during Christmas and emptied his pockets and given a needy person his last dime.

God says he sees a mighty man of valor. I wanted you to get to know my son Howard. I am so proud of him and his hard work and sacrifices made to help me. I think I can rightly say most guys his age would not live in a town where they knew no one simply because he wanted to watch out for his mother.

Howard means leader… and he has a very caring heart. Howard has had many struggles in life but he is not a victim, he is victorious. I hope and pray the Lord will give Howard the desires of his heart and he will find true purpose in life. He loves Jesus and assures me of that fact.

The Lord says we are to abide in him. Abide… means to remain, to reside, to await, to endure, to live up to a promise, to submit to and carry out. God wants a broken and contrite heart. Pride causes fallow ground of the heart.

FEAR…means False Evidence Appearing Real. Today if you are feeling anxious or worried, let's just take that to the throne room of God. He said cast all your cares, fears and concerns, worries upon the Lord for he cares for you. In fact no one cares for us like Jesus. Your past does not dictate your future. We are all a work in progress.

SCRIPTURE PROMISE

If you abide in me and my word abides in you then you shall ask what you will and he will give it to you.

—JOHN 17:7

PRAYER

Dear Heavenly Father, thank you for Jesus who is the way, the truth and the life. Dear God, you have not given us a spirit of fear, but power and love and a sound mind. Your love helps us to conquer our fears... You do not want your children to be imprisoned by fear. You said in Psalm 34:3 "I sought the Lord and he heard me and delivered me out of all my fears". Fear not, "for I am with thee, be not dismayed for I am thy God: I will strengthen thee: yes, I will help you: yes, I will uphold you with the right hand of my righteousness." Isaiah 41:1O. Praise God, there is nothing that can separate us from your great love. Thank you for salvation, deliverance and a changed heart. In Jesus' name, we pray. Amen.

HOW TO CONTACT THE AUTHOR

To reach Jackie Holland, founder and President of Whosoever Will Outreach Ministry and Chaplains for Women International, both 501c3 non-profit organizations, with questions regarding speaking engagements, upcoming seminars, Media TV interviews

Contact Jackie at:
jackie@jackieholland.org
www.jackieholland.org

Or write to:
Whosoever Will Outreach Ministries
PO Box 57
Sherman Texas 75091

Follow Jackie on Facebook: Jackie (Jackson) Holland

Follow her also on Twitter :
jackiejacksonholland@whosoeverwill

Myself and my Sisters Marita and Barbara Ann

Jackie's Mom Elaine (Israel mission trip)

My son Howard and daughter Charlsey

Book sign of *Exposed Heart*
(Jackie's first book, Laquetta)

My son Howard

Jackie and Claudia, radio/tv program

My firstborn son Mike and myself

Howard and Dallas Cowboy owner Jerry Jones

Entertaining the Queen of Buganda
(Charlsey, Queen of Buganda, Jackie)

Jackie mission trip Africa

My daddy
Woodrow Jackson
and oldest son Mike

Dancers Outreach

Toys for Kids (Jackie)

Chaplain Jackie Holland

My son Howard and daughter Charlsey

Widows luncheon (Jackie and her mom Elaine)

My son Michael David, graduation

Jackie, ministry at strip club

Jackie at praise rally

My high school sweetheart and
first husband Charles and myself

My siblings: sisters Marita and Barbara Ann and brother Don

Prision Outreach

Do not despise
small beginnings

Whosoever Will donation check (Jackie, Tobra)